STURGEON
TARGET-TUG EXTRAORDINAIRE

Tony Buttler

Contents

Introduction 4

A Question of Asymmetry: *The Sturgeon Naval Bomber* 6

'The Most Luxurious Target-Tug': *The Sturgeon's New Rôle* 20

Long-Term Insurance: *The S.B.3 Anti-Submarine Aircraft* 36

Orthodox Form: *A Glimpse beneath the Sturgeon's Skin*   44

'A Gentlemanly Response': *The Sturgeon in the Air*   54

Target Matters: *The Sturgeon as a Fleet Requirements Aircraft*   60

Pulling, Not Pushing: *The Sturgeon in Squadron Service*   62

Colours and Markings: *A Selection of Short Sturgeon Paint Schemes*   81

Introduction

I was delighted when Roger Chesneau asked me to write this modest book on the Short Sturgeon, although seasoned aviation enthusiasts might wonder why such a relatively obscure aeroplane should be given such treatment. Surely books covering individual aircraft designs confine themselves to those that were a great success, those that were in the thick of wartime action, or those that for some reason proved controversial? The Sturgeon was first ordered as a naval bomber but in that form it never progressed beyond prototype flying. When production orders were placed (and then in relatively small numbers), they covered a variant designed for target-towing—a relatively humble occupation. Neither, with so few airframes built, did the Sturgeon have a prolonged career. So why a book? There is more to this than mere facts, and I offer the following reasons:

1. The Sturgeon bomber was a handsome machine and, with its contra-rotating propellers and other features, technically of some interest.
2. In the air the aircraft flew well—and, fortunately, some of the aircrew who operated the target tugs are still with us. It is well worth recording what they have to say about the aeroplane, and to those who were there the contribution made by the Sturgeon was of course very valuable.
3. The life of the target-tug and the people involved is one of the lesser known aspects of aviation history, and uncovering a little of what was involved has proved fascinating.
4. There was also an anti-submarine development of the Sturgeon which, rather unattractive though it was, introduces an element of 'what might have been'.
5. Finally, from my own point of view, it can be just as interesting researching and writing about these 'lesser' types as it is covering aviation's more successful or spectacular aircraft.

I trust that the result gives some deserved credit to the Sturgeon and to the Fleet Air Arm personnel who flew and maintained her. It does mean that the history of the aircraft is now better documented for posterity, and I hope that those who pick up this book find it as enjoyable to read as it was for me to put it together. The history of aviation is littered with minor or lesser-known types like the Sturgeon, and perhaps some readers might be inspired to dig into the history of more of these relatively obscure aeroplanes. I hope so!

As ever, even for a slim publication such as this one, there are many one must thank. First there is Roger Chesneau, for taking the plunge and asking me to undertake the project. Next, Ken Ellis kindly gave permission for me to revise and re-use some articles I had written for him a while ago when he was the editor of the sadly now defunct *Air Enthusiast* magazine; the original articles were compiled with the help of Joan Grenville and Ken Best at Bombardier/Short Brothers. Thanks are due also to Fred Ballam, Mick Burrow, Phil Butler, Gerry Fielding, Peter Green, Commander David Hobbs MBE, Phil Jarrett, Brian Lowe, Geoff

Wakeham and Dick Ward for their assistance in loaning photographs and other material, and to the staff of the National Archives, for their help in locating original documents relating to the Sturgeon and its development, and of the Fleet Air Arm Museum, for their assistance with illustrations. Michael Oakey, the editor of *Aeroplane*, generously gave permission for me to use several of the magazine's photographs, to extract portions of Derek Dempster's 1951 article on the Sturgeon, and to make use of some text from another *Aeroplane* article covering aspects of 'tugging' that was published in the 28 November 1947 issue. These were vital contributions.

Last but certainly not least, my profuse thanks go to the retired Fleet Air Arm officers with direct experience of the Sturgeon who have allowed us to tap into their memories to give us all a feel for what the aircraft was like: Commander Andy Phillip, Lieutenant-Commander (Operations) at RNAS Hal Far from 1953 to 1956; Commander David Corkhill DSC, who for a period was CO of 728 Naval Air Squadron; Commander Gordon Roberts OBE, who from 1951 to 1953 was 728 Squadron's Senior Observer and RNAS Hal Far's Station Photographic Officer; Commander Graeme Rowan-Thomson, Lieutenant-Commander Peter Dallosso, Lieutenant-Commander Andy Hamilton and Lieutenant Harry Hands, all of whom also flew with 728 Squadron; Lieutenant-Commander 'Cue' Cureton of 728 NAS (who, sadly, passed away as this book was in preparation); Lieutenant-Commander Peter Hiles from 703 Squadron; the hugely experienced Captain Alan Leahy CBE DSC; and, of course, the legendary test pilot Captain Eric Brown CBE DSC AFC. Also rendering considerable help, with his first-hand knowledge of Royal Navy shipboard gunnery systems, has been Sam Watson. I am most grateful to every one of them.

I must add that three Air-Britain publications—*The British Aircraft Specifications File* by Ken Meekcoms and Eric Morgan (Tonbridge, 1994), *The Squadrons of the Fleet Air Arm* by Ray Sturtivant and Theo Balance (Tonbridge, 1994) and *Fleet Air Arm Fixed-Wing Aircraft Since 1946* by Ray Sturtivant with Mick Burrow and Lee Howard (Tonbridge, 2004)—have been immensely valuable for the purposes of checking data and filling important gaps in knowledge.

Tony Buttler AMRAeS
Bretforton, September 2009

Above: Sturgeon Mk 2 TS476 makes a landing approach during carrier compatibility trials, June 1950.

A Question of Asymmetry

The Sturgeon Naval Bomber

THE period 1944 to 1948 was unique in British aviation history in that it saw the end of World War II, the consequent cancellation of many production orders and new aeroplanes, but the full introduction of the jet engine as the powerplant for new combat aircraft. These factors resulted in some potentially outstanding piston-powered types such as Martin-Baker's marvellous M.B.5 fighter having their programmes terminated, while aircraft like the Westland Welkin high-altitude fighter and the Bristol Buckingham bomber were built in numbers, delivered direct to storage and then very quickly scrapped without seeing squadron service. Had the jet aeroplane taken a few more years to reach fruition, then perhaps some of the piston types whose careers were abruptly curtailed might have figured more strongly in RAF and Fleet Air Arm history books. One of these aircraft could have been the Short Sturgeon.

In April 1943 a number of companies submitted projects to the new specification S.6/43, which called for a combined naval torpedo bomber and reconnaissance aircraft. Short Brothers offered two projects, while Armstrong Whitworth and Fairey competed with twin-engine designs fitted with Rolls-Royce Merlins. Westland tendered an aircraft design featuring a single Napier Sabre piston engine. The two proposals from Shorts, submitted for approval in the summer of 1943, showed one aircraft powered by a single Bristol Centaurus radial and the other by two Merlins each driving contra-rotating propellers.

In due course S.6/43 was split into two—a torpedo bomber to O.5/43, which was eventually satisfied by the Fairey Spearfish, and a reconnaissance type. The latter again brought forth several proposals, including, this time, a jet project from Armstrong Whitworth, but all were rejected in favour of Short's twin-Merlin RM.14.SM design. Specification S.11/43 was written to cover three prototypes of this design and issued to the company on 12 February 1944 with Operational Requirement OR.146. The document actually classified the type as a prototype for visual reconnaissance and shadowing, by day or night, but one 1,000-pound bomb or four depth charges were to be included as a payload. Propellers were to be fully feathering, provision for the subsequent installation of Rolls-Royce Griffon engines was requested, and facilities for Rocket-Assisted Take-Off Gear (RATOG) were also required. Two 0.5in machine guns were to be carried, with provision for two more. It was specified that the aircraft's all-up weight should not exceed 24,000 pounds, and its best performance had to be achieved between sea level and 15,000 feet. There were to be three crewmen. An Instruction to Proceed was given in October and Shorts called the type the S.38; it was later renumbered S.A.1 in the Society of British Aircraft Constructors' universal postwar numbering scheme.

Below: The very first Sturgeon. Work on building the three prototype aircraft began at Rochester but only RK787, depicted, was completed here, flying from the manufacturer's airfield on 7 June 1946; following the merger of Short Brothers (Rochester & Bedford) Ltd and Short and Harland Ltd—to form Short Brothers & Harland—all design and production work on the Sturgeon was transferred to Queen's Island, Belfast.

COURTESY PHIL BUTLER

7

COURTESY PHIL BUTTLER

COURTESY PHILIP JARRETT

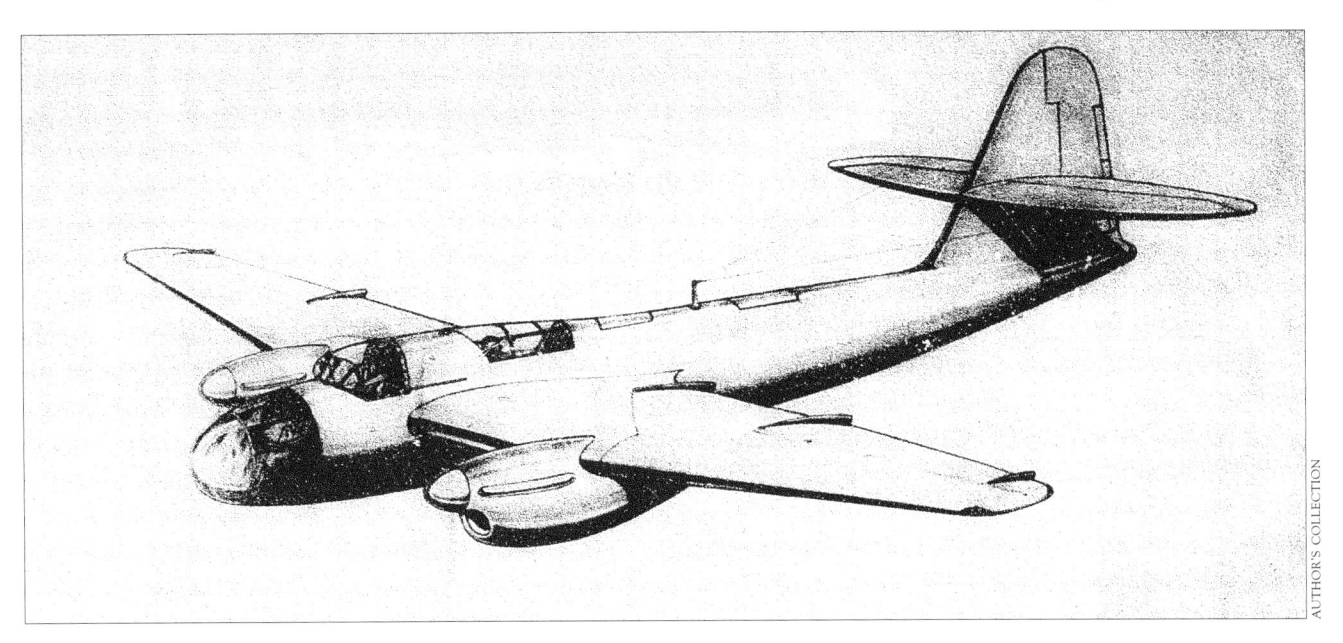

A QUESTION OF ASYMMETRY

Above: What the Sturgeon could have looked like. Fairey's competing design to S.6/43 was this twin Merlin-powered aircraft, which was expected to have a top speed of 341mph at 17,000 feet.

At the time, preparations were in hand for the final drive against Japan in the Pacific, and three prototypes were ordered to Contract No SB.27016/C.20(a) of 19 October 1943 with the serials RK787, RK791 and RK794. The aircraft was officially known as the Sturgeon S. Mk 1, with 'S' now standing for 'Strike'. However, RK794 was modified to Mk 2 target tug standard with a new serial VR363 (see below, page 20 *passim*). (The Sturgeon is of course a large fish from which caviar and isinglass are obtained. Some published sources have called the Mk 1 the F.R. Mk 1 and others have referred to it as the P.R. Mk 1)

The prototypes suffered delays during their construction. On 16 July 1945 a Ministry of Aircraft Production (MAP) representative visited Shorts' Rochester factory and reported that the first Sturgeon was in the very early stages of assembly. Part of the body had been tied to the centre wing section to which the engine nacelle structure had also been assembled, but there was clearly no hope of the aircraft being ready for flight by September (which presumably had been the planned date). The second prototype was about three months behind the first and the visitor urged an acceleration of this machine to cover any possible accident with RK787. His report also discussed the Griffon, but this engine was now unlikely to be fitted since its development was eighteen months behind that of the Merlin. The Griffon could be attractive for a target-towing aeroplane, and consideration was also being given to high-lift wings with full-span flaps.

In fact the first Sturgeon, RK787, made its maiden flight from its Rochester birthplace on 7 June 1946 in the hands of Geoffrey Tyson. The Short Brothers design team was led by C. P. T. Lipscombe and the works team came under the overall control of D. E. Wiseman, Shorts' Managing Director. These prototypes were the first twin-engine aeroplanes to be specifically designed for Fleet Air Arm service, although by the time the first example flew two de Havilland products originally produced for the RAF, the Mosquito and Hornet, had found their way on to the deck of an aircraft carrier.

Opposite page: Three photographs from a series of 'walk-around' views of the Short Sturgeon S. Mk 1 prototype RK787 taken at Rochester in June 1946. While arguably not sleek, the lines of the Sturgeon prototype exuded strength and purpose. The blunt nose of the aircraft was considerably extended when the design was adapted for target-towing duties but would be revisited in the final version of the Sturgeon, the T.T. Mk 3. In these photographs, the marginal sweepback of the leading edges of the outer mainplanes has masked the gentle dihedral that the wings certainly featured.

9

Both the Hornet and the Mosquito highlighted a major problem afflicting twin-engine aircraft landing on aircraft carriers—that of controlling it during the high-power/low-speed approach should one of the engines fail. Because of this inherent potential asymmetry the conventional Mosquito could not be deck-landed on one engine, while both propellers rotating in the same direction gave the added problem of swing on take-off. The Hornet and the naval Sea Hornets that followed were fitted with handed propellers that removed the problem of torque, but the question of asymmetry remained. It was hoped that the Sturgeon might prove better suited for single-engine landings since the shorter blades of its contra-rotating propellers allowed the engines to be placed closer to the fuselage centreline, thereby, theoretically, reducing the asymmetric tendencies.

On 26 June 1946 RK787 went to Farnborough for its first public display at the four-day British Aircraft Exhibition, and further appearances followed in early September at the SBAC Show at Radlett. On 25 April 1947 it joined 'A' Flight at the Royal Aircraft Establishment at Farnborough for arrester gear trials, and it was here that test pilot Captain Eric Brown evaluated the aeroplane. He found however, that on an asymmetric approach the lateral control with one engine was

Right: Sturgeon bomber prototype RK787 runs up its Merlin engines at Rochester Airport. Below: By employing contra-rotating propellers and short blades, and by positioning the powerplants close to the fuselage—these features are evident in this photograph of RK787—the Sturgeon's designers went some distance towards addressing the seemingly intractable problem of asymmetry, but even the renowned test pilot Captain Eric Brown considered that it would be unwise for a Sturgeon pilot to attempt a single-engine landing on board an aircraft carrier (see pages 58-59).

A QUESTION OF ASYMMETRY

insufficient to bring the speed down to acceptable limits for a landing. This problem of asymmetry was never truly solved until twin-jet powered aircraft became available with engines placed much closer to the centreline. However, the arresting proofing trials were near faultless thanks to the considerable strength built into the airframe, overall control response was good and the machine seemed well suited for its intended rôle. Captain Brown discusses his findings more fully on pages 58–59.

On 8 May RK787 was taken to the Aeroplane and Armament Experimental Establishment at Boscombe Down for more testing, including deck-landing trials on the 19th on board the aircraft carrier HMS *Illustrious*. In early September it again took part in the SBAC Show at Radlett, before re-joining the RAE for handling trials and then the A&AEE for another deck-landing assessment, this time after receiving some modifications at Rochester. However, on 8 October it crash-landed on *Illustrious*'s deck of after missing the wires: the aircraft's wing tip touched the ship's island and then it nosed over. The wreckage was transferred to RNAS Ford for examination and later returned to Rochester, where on 4 April 1948 authority was given for the airframe to be struck off charge and held as a source of spares for the second prototype. The remains were still at Rochester in the early 1950s.

The construction of the second machine, RK791, was begun at Rochester but completed in Belfast since the company was in the process of relocating. The part-built airframe was shipped to Northern Ireland in mid-1947, and RK791's first flight did not take place until 18 May 1948, when test pilot J. S. Booth took off from Sydenham airfield, adjacent to the Belfast factory. On 16 June the machine achieved its first landing on the carrier HMS *Implacable* during arrester gear trials. In mid-October it was allocated to 703 Squadron at RNAS Lee-on-Solent, the Service Trials Unit, for powered wing-folding tests on board HMS *Illustrious*, and then, until the year's end, was employed in catapulting and arresting trials and undercarriage strain gauge work at both the RAE and Belfast. On 2 February 1949 RK791 was loaned to the manufacturers so that it could be taken on test flights by Wing Commander Maurice Smith of *Flight* magazine and Mr R. G. Worcester from *The Aeroplane*.

From 27 to 29 April 1949 the RAE used RK791 to carry out some proofing trials from the BHV catapult installed at Farnborough. Two sets of tests were

Below and right: RK787 took part in both the 1946 and 1947 SBAC Shows. For the 1946 display the magazine *The Aeroplane* organised a series of publicity photographs, two of which are reproduced here. In the illustration at right, it can be discerned that the observer's station is occupied.

made, the first at an all-up weight of 19,000 pounds with the wing fuel tanks only partially full and the second at 21,700 pounds with full tanks, and these all proved satisfactory. RATOG trials followed at the RAE in late July, and then the aircraft was loaned again to Shorts, this time to participate in the National Air Races held at Elmdon Airfield near Birmingham from 30 July to 1 August. The prototype was entered by Rear-Admiral Slattery (the Managing Director of Short Brothers) and was to be flown by test pilot Tom Brooke-Smith in both the Air League and Kemsley Trophy Races. However, it was withdrawn from the latter to allow Brooke-Smith to fly the Short Sealand flying boat in the Final of the King's Cup. RK791's racing number for the event was '80'.

The Air League Challenge Cup Race was restricted to piston-engine aircraft with a sea-level top speed in excess of 250mph. The competitors were handicapped against their potential speed so that they started their laps around the fixed course at different times but would, it was hoped, arrive over the line at roughly the same time in a 'bunched' finish. Time was won or lost according to how well the pilots kept to the course and made their turns, and the event was won by Peter Lawrence in the Blackburn Firebrand. The Sturgeon recorded an

Below: RK787 makes a landing on board HMS *Illustrious*, 19 May 1947. The Sturgeon was not the first twin-engine aircraft to land on board an aircraft carrier, this achievement belonging to the de Havilland Mosquito, which had come on board HMS *Indefatigable* some three years earlier.

average speed of 295mph and at the end of the first lap it was in second place, 'smoking and noisy but doing well', but it was eventually overhauled by the Spitfire and (possibly) by the de Havilland Hornet.

More RATOG trials with 'A' Flight RAE began on 30 August, but on 13 December RK791 suffered damage to its starboard propeller, undercarriage and wing tip when a manhole cover on the airfield collapsed. Six months later it was declared surplus to CS(A) requirements and sent to RNAS Yeovilton for ground instruction purposes, being dispatched from Farnborough on 23 June. By December 1953 the fuselage was on the dump at Yeovilton, although the wings of RK791 were noted as being in store at Rochester in November 1954. The career of the bomber Sturgeon had failed to progress beyond these two prototypes.

In 1945 Short Brothers looked into the possibility of substituting the Sturgeon's Merlin powerplants with two Rolls-Royce AJ.40 jet engines to produce the

Above: The second Sturgeon prototype, RK791, prepares for the Air League Challenge Cup Race, summer 1949, complete with racing number on nacelles and tailfin.

Right: Another of the publicity pictures of RK787 by *The Aeroplane*. From this and other views, it would seem that the undersurfaces of the wings and tailplane were painted yellow, with the movable surfaces left in natural finish.

Below: RK787 executes a fast, low pass.

A QUESTION OF ASYMMETRY

Above, below and opposite: Further views of RK787 from *The Aeroplane*'s archives. The aircraft did not survive for long: some sixteen months after its first flight, it was damaged in a deck landing accident on board HMS *Illustrious* on 8 October 1947 when its arrester hook failed and was, as a result, struck off charge.

Short Sturgeon Mks 1–3 and S.B.3 Specifications

Manufacturer: Short Brothers (Rochester & Bedford) Ltd, Rochester, Kent; later Short Brothers & Harland Ltd, Queen's Island, Belfast.
Chief Designer: C. P. T. Lipscombe (Assistant Designer S. G. Hart).
Powerplant: (Mks 1–3) two Rolls-Royce Merlin 140 each developing 2,080hp, (S.B.3) two Armstrong Siddeley Mamba turboprops each developing 1,475shp.
Dimensions: Length overall (Mk 1) 44ft 0in (13.41m), (Mk 2, unfolded) 48ft 10in (14.88m), (Mk 2 folded) 44ft 9⅖in (13.65m), (Mk 3) 42ft 1in (12.95m), (S.B.3) 44ft 9in (13.56m); wing span (all) 59ft 11in (18.26m) spread, (Mk 1) 20ft 0in (6.10m) folded, (Mk 2, Mk 3) 22ft 5in (6.83m) folded;* height (all, folded) 15ft 3½in (4.66m); wing area (all, gross) 560.4 sq ft (52.06m^2); wing thickness/chord ratio (all) 15%; wing aspect ratio (all) 6.38; tailplane span (all) 20ft 0in (6.10m).
Weights: Normal (Mk 1) 21,700lb (9,845kg), (Mk 2) 22,000lb (9,980kg), (S.B.3) 23,600lb (10,705kg); maximum (Mk 1) 23,000lb (10,435kg), (Mk 2) 22,350lb (10,140kg), (Mk 3) 22,050lb (10,000kg).
Armament: (Mk 1, projected) Two or four 0.50in Browning machine guns plus 1,000lb (454kg) payload (bombs or depth charges) in bomb bay and sixteen 60lb (27kg) rocket projectiles underwing, (Mk 2, Mk 3) none, (S.B.3) up to 2,620lb (1,190kg) payload.
Performance: Maximum speed (Mk 1) 348kts (401mph, 645kph) at 18,850ft (5,750m),† (Mk 2) 319kts (367mph, 591kph) at 24,200ft (7,375m), (Mk 3) 318kts (366mph, 589kph), (S.B.3) 278kts (320mph, 515kph); rate of climb (Mk 1, at 20,000lb, 9,060kg, gross weight) 4,180ft/min (1,275m/min) at 2,000ft (610m) and 1,600ft/min (490m/min) at 28,000ft (8,530m), (Mk 2, at 19,500lb, 8,845kg, gross weight, not towing) 2,800ft/min (850m/min) at sea level‡ and 1,960ft (595m) at sea level towing a 32ft (9.75m) winged target; service ceiling (Mk 1, at 20,000lb) 35,700ft (10,880m), (Mk 2, at 19,500lb) 35,200ft (10,730m); maximum ceiling (Mk 1, at 20,000lb) 38,000ft (11,580m); take-off run (Mk 1, at 20,000lb) 630ft (192m) in still air or 240ft (73m) in 27kt (31mph, 50kph) headwind, (Mk 2, at 19,500lb) 750ft (230m) in still air or 180ft (55m) in 31mph headwind.
Number built: 28 (4 prototypes, 23 Mk 2s, 1 S.B.3; 19 Mk 2s later converted to Mk 3).

* The reason for the discrepancy between the figure for the folded width of the Mk 1 and that for the same dimension of the Mks 2 and 3 is not clear, but it may be that the larger figure refers to the *maximum* folded width, i.e., when the outermost propeller blades of each engine were in the horizontal plane.
† Some sources quote 430mph at 19,000ft (5,790m). Several of the 'official' figures relating to the Sturgeon's performance are at variance with one another.
‡ Some Shorts documents quote 2,470ft (750m) at sea level.

Left: RK787 reveals its undersides in a steep bank to port. The somewhat limited extent of the bomb bay, designed to accept a 1,000lb load, can just be made out. There was no requirement for the aircraft to carry a torpedo.

Fleet Air Arm night fighter shown in the drawings opposite. Information is scarce, but the aircraft's span would have been 61.9 feet, its folded span 22 feet 4.5 inches, its length 46.5 feet, its tailplane span 20 feet and its gross wing area 590 square feet, with a wing thickness:chord ratio of 14.9 per cent at the root and 15.6 at the tip and an aspect ratio 6.49. The estimated all-up weight was 23,500 pounds, and four 20mm cannon were to be mounted in the lower nose. There were nine fuel tanks, six in the wings taking up the space vacated by the leading-edge radiators of the old piston powerplant and holding a total of 546 gallons and three in the fuselage behind the cockpit with another 364 gallons, to give a total of 910 gallons.

It appears that this jet fighter was associated with the de Havilland Sea Hornet N.F. Mk 21 programme. When the idea for turning the basic Sea Hornet day fighter into a night fighter came under consideration, there was some concern that all of the equipment needed to operate it as such would not fit easily into the Hornet's slim airframe. The only alternative would be a development of the Sturgeon, which offered more fuselage space and therefore, as one document declared, could be more 'lavishly equipped'. However, the piston Sturgeon's

Right: Short Brothers' Drawing No CR.2842, showing the proposed Fleet Air Arm night fighter development of the Sturgeon of 1945, powered by two Rolls-Royce AJ.40 turbojets.

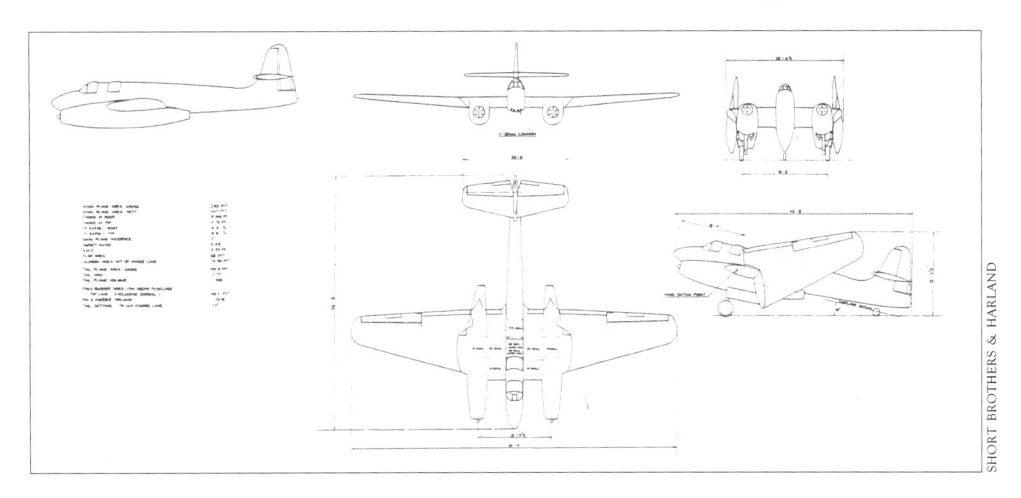

Right: Shorts' Drawing No CR.2842, showing how, in the 'Jet Sturgeon', the engine nacelles would still have housed the main undercarriage legs.

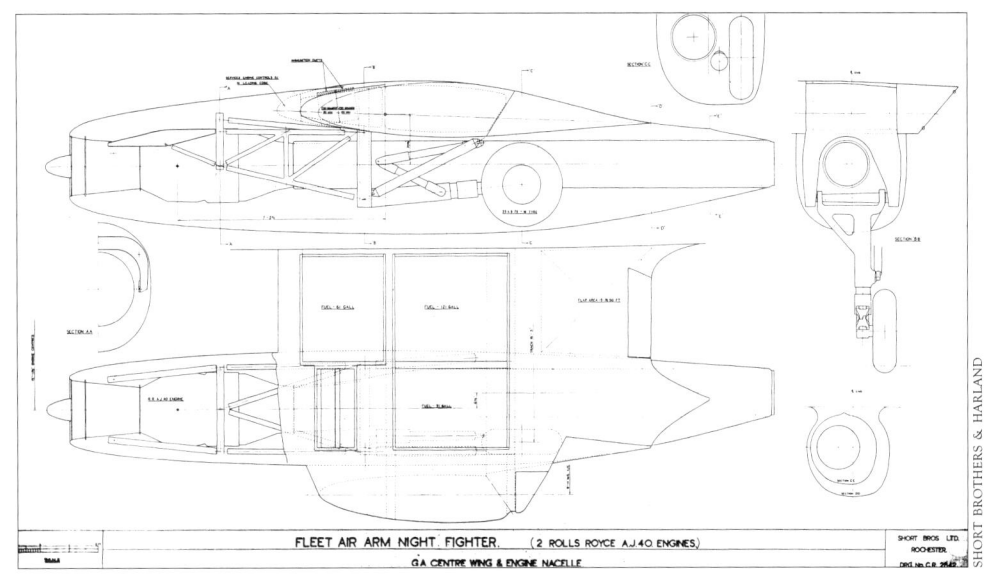

performance fell far short of the Sea Hornet's and in fact well short of the specified requirements as well. It was also felt at the time that the weaknesses in the Short Brothers' organisation would likely make the development of the Sturgeon bomber comparatively slow when the Staff at de Havilland was not only well organised but 'highly enthusiastic and anxious to proceed with this project.' Nevertheless, in June 1945 the company was asked to consider the design of a night fighter Sturgeon, and an official Admiralty document from early July noted that the new project 'would be very different from the Sturgeon in having more powerful engines which would be so installed that the arcs covered by the A.1 radar scanner (an essential feature of the night fighter) would be very much increased over what would be possible in the existing S.11/43.'

The 'Jet Sturgeon' drawing is almost certainly the competition that Short laid down against the night fighter Sea Hornet, and it would undoubtedly have offered more to the rôle than any piston development. However, official documents seem to confirm that the project ran only as an insurance in case the Sea Hornet proved more difficult to land on a carrier's deck at night than had been expected. Shorts' naval night fighter seems to have been examined in some depth. Its wings, body and empennage were quite similar to those of the Sturgeon, but the tail was placed higher on the fin to keep it clear of the jet exhaust. The Rolls-Royce designation AJ.40 stood for axial jet, 4,000 pounds' thrust. (The early non-RB prefixes were Rolls-Royce Derby designations while RBs came from Barnoldswick, but soon afterwards all jet engine projects were given RB numbers.) The Sturgeon jet fighter project was never ordered and the prototype Sea Hornet N.F. Mk 21 flew on 9 July 1946 and duly entered service.

'The Most Luxurious Target-Tug'

The Sturgeon's New Rôle

THE Sturgeon had been designed essentially for operations in the Pacific against Japan, but when that conflict came to a close the Royal Navy was left with a new bomber and nowhere to use it. It had been intended to operate the aircraft from the forthcoming large *Malta*, *Audacious* and *Hermes* class aircraft carriers, but postwar economies were to result in the cancellation or suspension of these new ships, and in fact none of the survivors would commission before 1952. Thus the only possible home for the Sturgeon was the wartime *Illustrious* class fleet carriers or the smaller *Colossus* class light fleet carriers, but operating from the former would require the installation of a stronger arrester gear while the Sturgeon itself would have to remain on the deck at all times as it could not be struck down using the existing lifts.

Consequently, the Sturgeon reconnaissance bomber was not ordered into production, but before the war was over the type was adopted as a target-tug. It was realised that, once the war had ended, sustaining a high standard of naval gunnery, both surface-to-air and air-to-air, would require the procurement of a high-performance, carrier-borne tug, and at a comparatively low cost. Since the Sturgeon was a well-built aircraft with agreeable handling qualities, the airframe was considered to be the ideal choice for this modification. In fact, Wing Commander Maurice Smith of *Flight* was to describe it as 'the most luxurious target tug to be ordered for any Service'. (At this time, after its work on the Stirling bomber and Solent flying boat, Short Brothers' reputation for quality of manufacture was very high indeed. It was often said that the chief fault of the Stirling was that it was too well made, while the Solent was considered to be a 'Rolls-Royce' of civil flying boats.)

Below: The third prototype Sturgeon, RK794 (shown), was never completed as such but instead was redesigned as the prototype target-tug, shipped to Belfast in 1947 and given the new identity VR363; a second aircraft, VR371, was completed to a similar configuration for trials and testing.

Above: VR363 in the air. The aircraft's upper surfaces and fuselage sides have been painted—apparently in yellow; the under surfaces remain natural metal.
Below: VR363 runs up its engines preparatory to a take-off.

Conversion to T.T. Mk 2 configuration, which Shorts called the S.39 and then S.A.2, was undertaken to Specification Q.1/46 and Operational Requirement OR.225 dated 6 September 1946. These declared that the aircraft must perform the following duties: target towing for both ground-to-air and air-to-air firing practice by day or night; the photographic marking of towed target firings; and radar calibration. For cinema marking duties, a continuous speed of 260 knots was required at 15,000 feet, and the towing speeds needed for a 32-foot and 16-foot winged target and for a four-foot, low-drag sleeve were 260, 275 and 260 knots, respectively. A two-foot low-drag sleeve had to be towed at 280 knots at 15,000 feet, while the tug itself had to be capable of operating for up to two hours at a height of at least 30,000 feet. The Sturgeon needed to carry enough fuel to be able to tow a 32-foot target for three hours, one hour of which would be at a height of 15,000 feet. The winch fitted in the aeroplane was to be capable of providing a tow length of at least 6,000 feet, the aircraft itself had to be able to carry four four-foot and six two-foot targets, full night flying equipment was required and an electronic jammer was requested that was to be capable of jamming the Fleet's radars. The all-up-weight was not to exceed 22,000 pounds, and the crew would be composed of a pilot and a second man who doubled as winch-operator, marker, wireless-operator and navigator.

The biggest change from the original Sturgeon was the introduction of a much longer nose that housed a Vinten camera for photographing 'throw off' gunfire; the wing, engines and tail were little altered. The second man had to operate the drogue target equipment and the Miles power-driven hydraulic winch from a new position abaft the wings. When the winch was not fitted, he had to crawl under the pilot's seat to reach the nose compartment, the fuselage having been deepened slightly to make room. The winch replaced the S. Mk 1's reconnaissance camera installation.

We have already alluded to the plans for a third S.A.1 prototype, RK794, but during construction this aircraft was modified to act as the prototype T.T. Mk 2 and re-serialled VR363 under Contract No ACFT/5960/C.20(a) dated 25 July 1946. Work began on this machine at Rochester, but in the middle of 1947, when 70 per cent complete, the airframe was moved to Belfast. A second Mk 2 prototype, VR371, was also competed at Belfast, having been shipped from Rochester when around 20 per cent complete. VR363 made its maiden flight from Sydenham on 18 May 1948 and in September performed at the SBAC Farnborough Show. On 3 March 1949 authority was given for VR363 to be delivered to the Aeroplane and Armament Experimental Establishment, Boscombe Down,

Right: VR363 about to land at Sydenham following a test flight. This aircraft, the first of the pair of Sturgeon target-tug prototypes, was employed principally to test the aircraft's handling qualities in all its various flight regimes.
Below: The fourth Sturgeon prototype, and the second completed in target-tug form, VR371 concerned itself mainly with proving the on-board equipment—towing gear, photographic installations, etc. It first flew in April 1949 and enjoyed a decade-long career of flight-testing. It carries partial service markings in the form of a yellow band around the rear fuselage, though, interestingly, not the legend 'Royal Navy'.

'THE MOST LUXURIOUS TARGET-TUG'

for approval trials, which included deck landings on board *Illustrious* on 26 May that year.

VR363 was thoroughly tested at Boscombe Down between April and July, again in January 1950 and then from May to July 1950. The time gaps were, in part, required for repairs and modifications to be made to the airframe. For general handling the Sturgeon tug was considered easy and pleasant to fly, and suitable for the intended rôle, and the single-engine flying characteristics were good. A large change of trim when operating the radiator flaps had to be corrected with a modification by the manufacturers. It was considered that a single-engine deck landing could be made in an emergency by a pilot experienced in deck landings on the type, although a very high degree of judgement would be essential. A sinking approach was recommended as offering the greatest margin of controllability on the approach and at the 'cut'. A&AEE's pilots expected that the true approach speed would probably be in the range 107–115mph, i.e. up to 23mph faster than a normal deck landing.

Climb and level-speed performance tests were made using VR363 after the aircraft was fitted with Merlin 140S/1 engines, which differed in some important respects from the Merlin 140s fitted in production T.T. Mk 2s. At a take-off weight of 22,100 pounds, a maximum rate of climb of 2,030 feet per minute was measured up to the full throttle height (9,800 feet) in MS (medium supercharged) gear. Service ceiling was 34,800 feet and 34.5 minutes were taken to reach this height. At 21,000 pounds' weight and maximum continuous power, plus nine pounds boost in FS (fully supercharged) gear, a maximum cruising speed of 325mph (282 knots) was measured.

With a sleeve in tow the Sturgeon handled normally, but of course to avoid fouling the cable any turns, climbs or dives had to be shallow. The aircraft was never designed to be aerobatic, so figures for such as rate of roll were quite low, but normal landings were very comfortable. With the aircraft in clean condition, pilots were restricted to a maximum permissible speed of 415mph (360 knots). One of the specified limits for cinema marking duties had been a continuous 300mph (260 knots) at 15,000 feet but in fact VR363 was able to demonstrate 312mph (271 knots) at this height. Other results satisfied the requirements beautifully—the various targets could all be towed at 15,000 feet within a speed range of 300–319mph (260–277 knots). In trials, the normal ceiling was estimated to be 33,000 feet with no target, and 28,000 feet when towing the worst and most 'draggy' target.

In May 1951 *Flight* reported the handling procedure with a 32-foot winged target as follows. When the target had been secured the engines were cleared and the aircraft taxied slowly forward, as directed by the marshal, in order to take up the slack in the towing cable and to align for take-off. The normal cable length was 350 feet—a 'short tow'. After unsticking at about 98mph (85 knots), the aircraft was held down until the speed had built up to 127mph (110 knots), at which point the initial climb could begin and the speed would then increase to 138mph (121 knots) after the power settings were reduced to plus twelve pounds' boost and 2,850rpm. A sustained climb was made to 500 feet to get the target clear of obstacles: if an engine failed at this point, the winch operator would be ordered to cut the target adrift. The recommended speeds were: (i) for reeling out, 150mph

Below: As well as the obligatory flight-testing for Royal Navy Sturgeons, VR363 was employed as a tug for Shorts' experimental, private-venture S.B.1 tail-less glider, the original incarnation of the better-known, turbojet-powered 'Short Harland Experimental and Research Prototype Aircraft', or Sherpa. The first flight—which is seen under way here—occurred on 30 July 1951. See page 27.

Above: A study of VR363 as it originally appeared, with a yellow fuselage band and a 'C' Type fin flash out of keeping with its 'D' Type roundels. Notice the cut-out beneath the centre fuselage from which the towing cable was streamed; the production arrangement differed from that visible, in particular in having a spreader positioned immediately forward of the (retractable) tailwheel to prevent the cable snagging the wheel when the latter was in operation.

(130 knots); (ii) for reeling in, 115–121mph (100–105 knots) initially and then 127mph (110 knots) once the winch was operating; and (iii) for the 32-foot target, the climbing speed should be 150mph (130 knots). For landing, a ground controller passing instructions by R/T was really needed to assist the pilot. Speed was reduced to 115mph (100 knots), flaps were fully lowered and a long, straight approach was made from 800 feet, the rate of descent being regulated in accordance with the controller's instructions. The boundary would be crossed at about 300 feet and the descent continued until the target was released—which should be automatic when it touched the runway, although if it failed to do so the controller would order the winch operator to cut the cable.

The results of the trials showed that the T.T. Mk 2's behaviour and deck-landing and take-off characteristics were very similar to those of the F.R. Mk 1, but the elevator area had to be increased by approximately 20 per cent. This modification was tested in the set of trials with VR363 held in January 1950, and the reason behind the alteration to the elevator was to give the Sturgeon more control engine-off, at forward centres of gravity and at low airspeeds. This improved the aircraft's handling for a 'dead-stick' landing. When tested, VR363 lacked some of its internal equipment and so had to be ballasted to provide the required weight and CofG. Night flying was also found to be pleasant and easy, and the aircraft was considered acceptable for Service carrier operation.

The leading-edge profiles of the wing centre section had to be modified at the design stage to accommodate the requisite cooling duct entries. However, after early flight reports of low-speed instability, problems with control when landing and poor climb performance (and draughts down the pilot's neck), a systematic programme of entry lip development by flight test was initiated. The local airflow characteristics were verified by wool-tufting the wings while various forms of wooden lip shapes were each tried in turn. When the optimum shape had been determined, some remarkable improvements were revealed. The Sturgeon's low-speed instability had been eliminated, the control from the elevator had been improved, the rate of climb had gone up from 2,000 feet a minute to 2,800, the top speed rose by about 23mph (20 knots) and the stalling speed had been reduced from 85 to 78mph (74 to 69 knots) with a corresponding improvement in the deck-landing attitude. Finally, the pilots no longer complained of stiff necks! These results were a classic illustration of the benefits of aerodynamic refinement because they were all associated with improved airflow, both internal

Above: Compact Sturgeon: VR363 on board the trials carrier HMS *Illustrious* in May 1949. The propellers have been positioned so as to minimise the overall width of the aircraft when its wings are folded. The hinged nose section of the Mk 2 is clearly seen; as well as reducing the aircraft's length, this facility permitted access to the equipment within. The non-slip walkway along the starboard wing root, aiding the pilot's access to his 'office', is also evident in this photograph.

and external, through the radiators. The value of wool tufts in locating a region in which trouble lay was also highlighted.

On 1 February 1950 VR363 joined 703 Squadron at RNAS Lee-on-Solent as '089'. Following another period with A&AEE, on 14 June the prototype Mk 2 re-joined 703 to begin intensive flying trials on board *Illustrious*, only for it to be discovered that two different marks of Merlin had been fitted which prevented the throttles from being synchronised. The aircraft was thus rejected and not flown.

It had been planned to bring VR363 up to full service standard but in the end this was not done. The aircraft was loaned to Short Brothers on 26 and 27 May 1951 so that it could be towed through the streets of Belfast as part of the Festival of Britain celebrations, but afterwards the company was informed that the Service had no further use for it. However, the loan was extended to allow Shorts to use VR363 to tow the firm's S.B.1 glider, a small research aircraft fitted with an 'aero-isoclinic' wing (which had all-moving wing tips). The craft (B-serial G-14-5) was launched for the first time by winch on 14 July 1951, piloted by Shorts' Chief Test Pilot Tom Brooke-Smith. It made its first flight towed behind VR363 on 30 July (Jock Eassie was the Sturgeon pilot), but did not fly again until 14 October, during which flight it crashed. The S.B.1 airframe was later rebuilt as the S.B.4 Sherpa with its own power source in the form of two small jet engines. VR363 was no longer needed and its loan expired during the following March when the aircraft went into storage, before being rated Category 5 in October 1953 for reduction to 'spares and produce' (i.e., scrap).

Above: A Mk 2 viewed from head-on, showing the neatness of the wing-folding system. Notice that, although *contra*-rotating, the Sturgeon's propellers were not *counter*-rotating (i.e, they were not 'handed'); note, too, that the original arrangement for each engine in the prototype S.1 (see photograph across pages 10–11) was reversed in production Sturgeons. The sturdy undercarriage is also evident here: Short Brothers were very proud of this feature of their design—it was 'by far the strongest British unit which the Navy has yet used, and has been specially designed and constructed for the aircraft', according to company information brochures of the time.

Above: TS476, the second production Sturgeon T.T. Mk 2, prepares to take off from HMS *Illustrious* during deck-landing trials, June 1950.

Having made its first flight on or before 28 April 1949, and having since been fitted with its tug equipment, VR371's first job was target-towing and preliminary camera trials at the A&AEE in October 1949. On 24 January 1950 the prototype went to the Airborne Forces Experimental Establishment at Beaulieu for target-tug camera trials and again in July to clear the winch's hydraulic system. Later VR371 was used by Shorts at Belfast for preliminary work on modifications introduced to the Sturgeon in the light of service experience. In June 1955 it was used at the old Rochester site to carry out flight trials of some new automatic control equipment developed by Elliot Brothers, experiments which eventually lasted twelve months. VR371 was still at Rochester in 1957 and was finally sold for scrap on 22 January 1959.

A production batch of twenty-three aircraft was ordered with the serial numbers TS475–TS497, a series originally allocated to S. Mk 1s—which explains why these numbers precede that of the Mk 2 prototype. In all, thirty Mk 1s had been planned (TS475–TS504), and these were ordered under Contract No ACFT/4020/C.20(a) issued on 26 January 1945. The original contract was then cancelled in August 1946 and replaced by ACFT/5960, which covered ten examples of the S. Mk 1 plus eighteen Mk 2 tugs. In December this was amended to confirm that all 28 would now be built as tugs, and then on 10 November 1947 the order was reduced to 23, all to be built at Belfast. These aeroplanes made their first flights between 6 December 1948 (TS475) and 13 February 1952 (TS497). TS475 joined 703 Squadron at Lee-on-Solent on 28 October 1949 and conducted the first deck trials on *Illustrious* on 4 November. From February to June 1950 A&AEE trials were conducted with the T.T. Mk 2 towing two-foot and four-foot sleeve targets and 32-foot wing targets and the type's performance was found to be satisfactory. On 3 June the type was released to the Service but, for the time being, only for operation from land aerodromes and in temperate climates. The latter point was a result of some limitations in target-towing performance that had been revealed in tropical conditions.

TS476 was used for intensive deck landing trials between 19 and 23 June 1950 on HMS *Illustrious* at a maximum weight of 20,000 pounds. Afterwards RNAS Ford reported on 10 July that the aircraft was accepted for deck-landing in service with the proviso that landing on a badly pitching deck was likely to be hazardous on account of some problems with elevator control. A total of sixty test landings had been made, and it was also noted that, thanks to its large span, particular attention should be made to lining up the Sturgeon for take-off and landing on the centre-line. The A&AEE reported on 7 March 1951 that the Sturgeon target-tug was not completely satisfactory for unrestricted deck landing at a 20,000-pound landing weight owing to limitations in its undercarriage performance and the lack of adequate elevator control to assure a three-point touch-down. This was no longer particularly important, however, because from about August 1950 the Sturgeon's deck-landing requirement became secondary to aerodrome landing. Nevertheless, in late July/early August 1951 TS477, serving with 703 Squadron,

Above and below: Two photographs showing TS476 taking off from HMS *Illustrious*. These evaluations were conducted by the Service Trials Unit (703 Naval Air Squadron), based at RNAS Ford in Sussex.

This spread: Aspects of TS476 on carrier approach and landing. Notice, in the photograph opposite top, the vital Deck Landing Control Officer, or 'batsman', whose interpretation of the landing approaches of all Royal Navy aircraft at this time and resultant corrective signalling the pilot of the incoming aircraft was compelled to obey; and the planeguard destroyer, ready to race to the rescue in the event of an accident. In the photograph opposite bottom, deck handlers are rushing to secure the aircraft and, no doubt, re-spot it for another take-off—no time was wasted during Service trials! TS476's undersurfaces carry the standard target-tug finish of black diagonal striping over a yellow background.

'THE MOST LUXURIOUS TARGET-TUG'

COURTESY DAVID HOBBS/BRIAN LOWE

FLEET AIR ARM MUSEUM

THE AEROPLANE

31

Left: Among several revolutionary Navy-related British inventions of the 1950s was the steam catapult, the brainchild of Commander Colin Mitchell RNVR. The first such device, a prototype, was installed on board the light aircraft carrier HMS *Perseus*, and a large number of different aircraft types were test-launched from it. One was Sturgeon TS477 ('004'), which participated the trials in July–August 1951 and is seen here being readied for take-off from the carrier.

Left: TS477 is catapulted from *Perseus*. This new launching system consigned all earlier mechanical accelerating devices—and there were many different kinds—to history and was universally adopted throughout the world's navies; indeed, the conventional high-performance aircraft of today cannot operate at sea without its assistance.

Right: Three photographs of the first production Short Sturgeon T.T. Mk 2, TS475, taken at Sydenham on a rainy day in December 1948. The aircraft is, as shown here, not yet fully equipped.

undertook steam catapult trials aboard the experimentally rigged carrier HMS *Perseus*.

In service the Sturgeons went to shore-based establishments. In 1951 the Royal Navy ended 'throw-off' target practice and introduced radar gunlaying instead and the long-nose Sturgeon was therefore no longer required to work with the Fleet. In November 1953 discussions began between Shorts and the Ministry of Supply to modify Mk 2 aircraft with shorter noses as T.T. Mk 3s. Essentially, the tugs were simplified by having all the carrier equipment removed and a new nose—which in fact came close to the shape of the original Mk 1–fitted. Shorts called this variant the S.B.9 and, because of the workload at Belfast, the conversions were carried out by Shorts Flying Services Division at Rochester (which also performed the Sturgeon's overhauls). However, the first Mk 3, TS475, was converted at Belfast.

TS475 went to Belfast on 1 February 1954 for its conversion and to conduct flight trials with the short nose as the T.T. Mk 3 prototype; as such, it made its first flight on 21 May. On 18 June it arrived in Malta to begin overseas flight trials and in July joined 728 Squadron at RNAS Hal Far, Malta. In all, nineteen conversions were completed (far more than most published sources have indicated), the others being TS476–486, TS488, TS490, TS492, TS493 and TS495–497. The first flights in this form were made between 29 June 1954 (TS493) and 1957, and these aircraft continued to serve at Hal Far until they were withdrawn in 1958. Four Mk 2s did not survive to undergo conversion: TS487 was damaged during its delivery flight in July 1951, TS489 suffered an engine failure on take-off

'THE MOST LUXURIOUS TARGET-TUG'

STURGEON

Above, below and right: TS475, now equipped, painted and ready for delivery to the Navy; the aircraft has its full suite of communications equipment and towing devices, including the stays on the tailplane for rigging cables to prevent the towing line from fouling the control surfaces. A further photograph of TS475 in this configuration appears on the front cover of this book. In this form the aircraft entered service with 703 Squadron on 28 October 1949.

from Belfast on 27 September 1951, and TS494 ran off the runway during a take-off from Hal Far in August 1952. These three aircraft were subsequently struck off charge. TS491, the fourth unconverted airframe, continued in service as a Mk 2. All the surviving Sturgeons were scrapped in 1958–60, most of them either at Lossiemouth or in Malta. Sadly, no airframe remains are known to exist today.

In the 1950s the title 'target-tug' would usually evoke an image of some run-down, former front-line aircraft re-employed after rough-and-ready modifications, but the Sturgeon T.T. Mk 2 was far from answering that description. It was a fine aircraft which was large enough and sufficiently well equipped to do the job with a surprisingly good performance. Noise for the crew was a problem, but the airframes were all built to a very high standard. As a tug, the Sturgeon provided a valuable training facility for operational ships, combat aircraft and ground forces and for new or recommissioned warships in the process of working-up.

Below: TS475 was later returned to the manufacturers to became the 'prototype' T.T. Mk 3 conversion with the shorter nose. This photograph showing its new form was taken at Rochester on 19 October 1954. Ironically, the view forward for the pilot when taking off, landing and taxying was considerably improved—although any possibility that the Sturgeon would be required to operate from aircraft carriers had long since vanished.

Long-Term Insurance

The S.B.3 Anti-Submarine Aircraft

ONE final development of the Sturgeon demonstrated the inherent versatility of the airframe but also marked a conversion from a good-looking aircraft to one whose appearance was near-grotesque. This variant—which was never called a Sturgeon but was referred to instead as the S.B.3 or M.6/49, after the specification covering it—was initially proposed by Shorts as an interim anti-submarine warfare aircraft to help fill the gap while the Navy waited for the successful development of a dedicated ASW type. The latter was to be either the Blackburn B.54 or the Fairey Type Q (later called the Gannet), both of which were flown in September 1949 to Specification GR.17/45.

By the late 1940s the growing strength of the Soviet Navy as an ocean-going, 'blue-water' fleet was causing concern and steps were needed to counter it. One of the new requirements prepared as a consequence was Specification M.6/49, which covered a naval anti-submarine and reconnaissance aircraft to Naval Requirement NR/A.9 and Operational Requirement OR.275. On 20 December 1948 a meeting was held at the Admiralty to consider the need to order prototypes and the production of a Sturgeon converted into an anti-submarine type against this

Left and below: The other Navy ASW types under development at the same time as the S.B.3 were the Blackburn B.54 (upper photograph) and the Fairey Type Q. Fairey's design won the contest and entered service as the Gannet and the lower photograph shows the prototype, VR546.

Above: Hardly the epitome of pulchritude, but conceived in a hurry, the S.B.3 was a straight adaptation of the Sturgeon Mk 1 but was never proceeded with in earnest. The primer gives the airframe a very patchy appearance in this photograph of the aircraft taken during its maiden flight. Air-to-air images of the S.B.3 are few in number.

requirement. However, by then the new version was no longer considered an interim aeroplane and was also unlikely to be available to the Navy more than six months in advance of one of the dedicated types. It was noted that the converted Sturgeon's high all-up-weight would make it usable in only a minority of carriers and prevent it from being a direct competitor to the Blackburn or Fairey projects.

During the meeting it was acknowledged that there was a general ignorance of the best equipment and tactical methods needed for finding and 'killing' a submarine, and after much discussion it was decided that there was a good case for ordering prototypes of the Sturgeon for development work on these matters. The aircraft's layout, with its three crewmen grouped together in the nose, gave a distinct advantage as, for example, this offered a better view during a visual search. In fact, an important objective of the ASW development programme was to try out the forward-observer compartment layout in a twin-engine aeroplane. However, the Fifth Sea Lord made it clear that no production order could be placed at present, and that there was little likelihood that one would be forthcoming in the future. The prototypes would act as anti-submarine research and development aeroplanes, although the Sturgeon conversion would also offer a long-term insurance against a complete failure of either Blackburn's or Fairey's aircraft. In such a case, the Sturgeon would be extremely valuable, although its use would be limited because of its high weight. The Ministry of Supply agreed but saw no reason to expect that either of the other types would be a failure.

Specification M.6/49 was raised on 3 May 1949 and called for an aircraft capable of anti-submarine duties, including level- or glide-bombing, plus reconnaissance, in areas where no enemy fighters were expected. A minimum top speed of 265 knots (305mph) was requested, together with the ability to fly comfortably at a speed as far below 175mph (152 knots) as possible. The best performance had to come in the height band between sea level and 5,000 feet, and at the higher altitude the machine's endurance had to be at least three hours. A big mix of weapons—up to six depth charges, one 2,000-pound anti-submarine torpedo, anti-submarine bombs or eight 25-pound rocket projectiles, plus sonobuoys, markers and pyrotechnics (flares)—was requested in six optional loads, to permit the aircraft to perform the dual functions of strike and search. An ASV Mk XV radar with a large scanner was also specified.

At an MoS Advisory Design Conference held on 8 March 1949 it was proposed to take two Sturgeons from the production line and convert them for the ASW rôle. Owing to the need to get the weight lower than the target-tug's, the power-plant was switched from Merlins to 1,475shp Armstrong Siddeley Mamba ASM.3 turboprops. The two prototypes were to be produced as quickly and as cheaply as possible and were expected to fly in February and May 1950, respectively. However, these conversions were to cause designer C. P. T. Lipscombe some problems because RAE Farnborough predicted that the S.B.3 would be understrength and so would need some alterations. In particular, the undercarriage required a lot of redesign.

LONG-TERM INSURANCE

The Specification was issued to Shorts on 19 May 1949 and the project was examined by the RAF on 4 October, the day of the Mock Up Conference. Fitting the two Mambas, which had four-bladed propellers, made this the first Shorts aircraft to use turbine engines. Chief Designer David Keith-Lucas had a slight preference for wooden propellers because they would give less interference to the radar, but in the end it was agreed that metal propellers should be used. In fact, the ASV radar's scanning range was not affected by the propellers, but had the latter been made in wood then splintering would have been an extra hazard should they strike a carrier deck. The forward fuselage was extensively redesigned and bulged to accommodate the large scanner under the floor plus two radar operators in a cabin beneath and ahead of the pilot's cockpit. The result was not handsome, but the rest of the aircraft was similar to the T.T. Mk 2: the rear fuselage was unaltered and the aircraft used many of the same components. Weapons were to be housed in both the bomb bay and on underwing hardpoints, and the maximum weapon load totalled 2,620 pounds. The wing span remained the same but the new engines increased the overall length to 44 feet 9 inches. As noted, the name Sturgeon was no longer used.

A production Sturgeon airframe, construction number SH.1599 (the original serial is unknown), was turned into the first S.B.3 prototype, WF632, under Contract No 6/ACFT/3955, but the second prototype,

Below: WF632 in its Navy paintwork—Extra Dark Sea Grey and Sky Type 'S' ('duck-egg green'). The principal differences between this aircraft and the Sturgeon were its Mamba turboprops, its completely redesigned forward fuselage and it more capacious weapons bay. The 'Royal Navy' legend signifies intention rather than endorsement.

Above: WF632 at Sydenham, with various other Short Brothers products visible in the background—a Sturgeon Mk 2 (left) and Sunderland (beneath the S.B.3's port wing) and Solent (far right) flying boats.

WF636, was built from scratch. By mid-January 1950 the first aircraft had been delayed owing to an excessive number of design defects and also because of the effects of the company's move from Rochester to Belfast (this second point was considered a special factor and, indeed, did account for much of the delay). Finally, on 12 August 1950 WF632 was taken on a twenty-five minute maiden flight by Tom Brooke-Smith. At a take-off weight of 17,887 pounds, the machine left the runway in twenty seconds after a near equivalent run to that required by the T.T. Mk 2, and then climbed to an altitude of between 1,500 and 2,000 feet. The undercarriage stayed down throughout the flight (a lock prevented its retraction) and some wide circuits of the Shorts aerodrome were made at a radius of between ten and fifteen miles.

Three days earlier it had been estimated that, at a take-off weight of 21,700 pounds, the S.B.3 would achieve 303mph (263 knots) at sea level and 298mph (259 knots) at 20,000 feet, that its service ceiling would be 21,000 feet and that its sea-level rate of climb would be about 1,600 feet per minute. In fact, the S.B.3's top speed proved to be about 320mph (278 knots) and its maximum weight 23,600 pounds. During early trials WF632 showed a deficiency in longitudinal and directional stability at slow speeds over the range of CofGs, but Keith-Lucas confirmed that a cure would be a minor matter. However, in due course it was found that the jets, which exhausted through downwards-directed pipes, created a marked stability problem: because the Mamba was a jet, its thrust and efflux varied with the level of power needed, and this made the S.B.3 difficult to trim. In addition, the old problem of asymmetry precluded shutting down one engine to take the cruise endurance beyond three hours—one of the reasons for fitting jets in the first place. In general, the S.B.3 lacked the good handling characteristics of the Sturgeon. It was never to be assessed operationally.

Between 4 and 11 September the first prototype was loaned to Shorts for display at the 1950 Farnborough Show. The aircraft's flight testing was then resumed and by 30 November WF632 had flown for some twenty-six hours. By 29 December wind-tuft flying was in progress, and this was to be cleared by 2 January 1951, by which time some extended jetpipes would also be ready for installation. A letter dated 6 February 1951 from Shorts' Resident Technical Officer, John V. Roberts, noted that flight-testing had centred on stability trials and wool-tuft airflow investigation. Narrow-chord propellers had been received, but work was now held up by an unofficial strike which had begun on 18 January. This had also halted the construction of WF636. Armstrong Siddeley had been ready to deliver the second aircraft's two Mambas but a bracing strut had fractured during a bench test and, consequently, some redesign was needed to help dampen the vibration.

However, on 11 April 1951 it was decided that all work on the M.6/49 programme should cease. The strike had been settled on 19 March but no further work had been undertaken on WF632 bar the fitting and flight-testing of some experimental modified leading edges to the wing outer section, which brought no change in the aircraft's stability characteristics. The aftward extensions to the tail pipes were now fitted and tests were due to commence, but WF632 made its last flight on 23 April. No work was done on WF636 between 6 February and 19 March and very little afterwards, and although its Mambas were ready for delivery they had not been received and the allotment for them had been cancelled.

A final progress report made on 16 May 1951 noted that the tailpipe extension had showed no improvement in the aircraft's stability characteristics and, because the Ministry contract had been terminated, Shorts had decided against further flight trials under the company's own responsibility. Allotments for the return of WF632's Mamba engines to Armstrong Siddeley had been cleared and one unit had already been removed. No work had been done on WF636 because of the cancellation of the contract, despite its being near complete in regard to mountings, wiring and installations. WF632 was accepted off contract on 21 June without the Contractor's Flight Trials being completed, a total of 39 hours 50 minutes' flying having been accumulated. After WF632 was reallocated to the firm in August 1951, Shorts made a request in October to break up the aircraft, and dismantling had commenced by 30 November. Spare parts were recovered for T.T. Mk 2s, with the residue disposed of as scrap, and WF632 was struck off charge on 3 January 1952.

WF636 was to have been used for tactical trials, for which it would carry sonobuoys and receive an ASV Mk 15 radar with a Type 77 scanner. Discussions

Below: The S.B.3 retained the Sturgeon's impressive wing folding capability. This photograph was taken at Sydenham in April 1951. The revised jetpipes evident in this view and the photograph opposite are noteworthy and may be compared with those shown elsewhere in this chapter.

STURGEON

held in early October 1950 had agreed that drop trials of a dummy Pentane anti-ship/anti-submarine torpedo should be carried out, along with tests on a new British non-directional sonobuoy that required service and tactical trials. (Pentane was the air-launched, passive-homing, 21-inch-diameter Mk 21 torpedo developed by Vickers/Whitehead for ASW aircraft like the S.B.3 and Gannet. It was too big and heavy for helicopters and was eventually cancelled.) However, by 1 November the second prototype had been held up by the non-availability of its powerplants and Shorts had had to use the spare engine from the first prototype as a slave to enable the plumbing and cowling to proceed. By 30 November the aircraft was ninety per cent complete, and the engines finally reached the maker's test-bed in January 1951. They were expected to be despatched to Short Brothers by the middle of that month, but in the end WF636 was never completed and was also swiftly broken up, again to supply spares for Mk 2 tugs. It was the Fairey Gannet that became the Navy's new anti-submarine warfare aircraft, and this custom-built type entered service in 1955.

Opposite page: Further portraits of the sole completed S.B.3. It is not known why the port and starboard propeller blades carried differing surface finishes.
Above: The S.B.3 airborne at Farnborough at the SBAC show in September 1950.
Below: The aircraft taking off at Farnborough for a display. The second S.B.3, WF636, was never completed and both airframes were ultimately broken up, suitable components being retained as spares for Sturgeons.

Orthodox Form

A Glimpse beneath the Sturgeon's Skin

THE Short Sturgeon S. Mk 1 naval reconnaissance-bomber was a very clean aeroplane. It had a laminar-section, two-spar, cantilever wing which was made in three pieces with heavy-gauge light alloy booms and plate webs. The constant-chord centre section passed right through the fuselage (and was built integrally with it) and there were two tapered folding outer planes which, as fitted, had 3.75 degrees of dihedral and 2 degrees of incidence. Stressed-skin construction was used, with special pre-stretched panels forming the leading-edge covering. Frise-type ailerons with spring tabs were employed, while a small trim tab for adjusting on the ground was fitted to the inboard end of each aileron. Trimming in flight was achieved by a differential action applied to the aileron control circuit. Zapp split trailing edge flaps were installed, these having sliding noses and upper-surface links that gave high drag plus an increase in the wing area. The all-metal ailerons were built up from a single spar with ribs of light alloy sheet and a light alloy riveted skin, while the spilt flaps were divided into four parts to allow the wings to fold, one outboard and one inboard of each engine nacelle.

The all-metal monocoque fuselage was built in four pieces with a stressed light alloy skin riveted to a skeleton of longerons and stringers. (On the T.T. Mk 2 tug the front section extended from the nose to Frame 7, the centre from Frame 7 to 10, the rear main section from 10 to 21 and the tail section from 21 to the tail.) Both tail and fin used spanwise stringers and two-spar construction and were built integral with the rear fuselage structure, and the elevators and rudder used combined servo trim tabs. The elevator surfaces were metal-covered from the nose to their light alloy spar, but aft of the spar they were fabric-covered. The rudder, too, had metal covering forward of the spar and fabric aft, and its combined trim-cum-servo tab extended along 53 inches of the lower rudder's trailing edge. Unlike the elevators, which were inset, the rudder had a horn balance.

The undercarriage was by far the strongest British unit yet employed and was designed to cope with a descent rate close on 16 feet per second when the specified rate was about 14. Wartime experience had shown that the lower figure was ample for all normal requirements, but the Navy had become exasperated by the inability of aircraft undercarriages to withstand the loads likely to be imposed on their structure in any kind of swell; as a result, the Service had pressed

Below: A three-quarter rear view of RK787 at Rochester in June 1946. The large, encircled 'P' was a standard marking for all British prototype aircraft, while other points of interest include the non-slip panelling giving the pilot a firm foothold en route to the cockpit; the 'blown' glazing at the observer's station, affording him some degree of outward visibility forward and aft; and the red/blue Type 'B' roundels on the upper wing surfaces.

its aircraft designers to deal with this problem. The Sturgeon's impressive long-stroke undercarriage units retracted into the underside of the engine nacelles, while the tail wheel was of the levered suspension type and was also retractable.

Power came from two Rolls-Royce two-stage, two-speed, supercharged Merlin 140 engines housed in underslung tubular nacelles close inboard to the fuselage; the intercoolers were underneath the engines. The Merlins were rated at 1,660hp for take-off and a maximum 2,080hp at 2,000 feet, and each drove a contra-rotating Rotol propeller with six wooden blades; wood was chosen because it minimised any interference suffered by the Type 77 air-to-surface vessel (ASV)

Above: The Sturgeon's area-increasing Zapp trailing-edge flap system is revealed in detail in this photograph of Mk 2 prototype VR363. Notice the crew access ladder and the observer's now flush side windows, his view of the outside world having been considerably enhanced by dint of the glazed cupola atop the fuselage.

STURGEON

ORTHODOX FORM

The Sturgeon's wing fold mechanism is demonstrated in this splendid portrait of the bomber prototype RK787 and shows just how well the aeroplane could 'tuck itself in'. The production target-tug retained the mechanism, which no doubt proved useful on occasion when stowing the aircraft in land-based hangars if not those below deck on board carriers. The engine panelling on the port nacelle has been removed; and notice, too, the plated-over machine-gun ports beneath the nose.

Rebecca IV radar scanner in the aircraft's nose. The contra-props were 10 feet in diameter and, being shorter than usual, helped the design to meet the difficult 20-foot folded width requirement. They gave the added advantage of eliminating swing on take-off.

On the S. Mk 1 and T.T. Mk 2 prototypes the blades of the front and rear units of the contra-rotating propellers were originally phased to cross at a point where they were nearest to the sides of the fuselage, but the noise levels thereby produced forced an alteration to this position by 30 degrees. When the Mk 2 prototype VR363 was first tested by A&AEE, the noise in the nose compartment caused by the vibration was so severe that, on several occasions during the trials, it brought about a complete failure of the intercommunication system. The re-phasing of the contra-rotating propellers so that the front and rear blades passed when 30 degrees away from the fuselage sides brought a marked improvement to the noise and vibration level in the cockpit, but the noise level at all crew stations was still high by customary standards of comfort.

The provision of power-folding wings to the 20-foot limit presented a difficult problem but Shorts came up with a unique and ingenious solution. Located towards the rear spar was a wing-folding hinge-pin and it was about this that the movement occurred. The hinge-pin was inclined at an angle of 47 degrees outward and was also set at an angle towards the rear of the aircraft. Thus, when operated by the hydraulic wing-folding jack, the wings would sweep downwards and back-

Below: Some of the innards of the port engine nacelle revealed. The Merlin 140s were equipped with automatically indexing cartridge starters, operated from the cockpit. The wings could be folded by activating a push-button when the engines were turning and hydraulic power was available; otherwise, a specially designed hand-pump was utilised.

wards. The rear spar was staggered 45 degrees at the wing root joint in order to allow this to happen, the outer wings folding rearwards in about ten seconds with the leading edge facing downwards (see illustration across pages 46–47).

Coolant radiators and oil coolers for each engine were installed in series in a wing duct between the engine nacelles and the fuselage. These were designed by Shorts using advice from RAE Farnborough, and the cooling air entered at the wing leading edge and was exhausted through a spanwise exit slot on the undersurface of the wing. The area of the exit was controlled by a flap hinged at its leading edge to the wing undersurface. Shorts also designed the arrester gear, with RAE assisting with the development of the hook; the latter was placed in a position at the extreme rear of the fuselage which was described as 'semi-sting', i.e., as far aft as possible but not actually protruding beyond the tail.

The S. Mk 1 had three crew members. The pilot was seated in line with the wing leading edge behind a laminated, bullet-proof windscreen and beneath a moulded bubble-type cover which slid backwards for access, the observer was in an armoured station in the fuselage ahead of the wing trailing edge, and the radio operator was situated immediately aft again. The armament comprised two 0.5in machine guns mounted in the lower nose with a total of 600 rounds of ammunition, eight rocket projectiles under each wing, and one 1,000-pound bomb, two 500-pound bombs or four 250-pound depth charges in the small bomb bay. The guns were not installed in the first prototype and the ports were covered over. An

Below: Details of the wing centre-section, with the engine mountings absent, the photograph conveying a good impression of the Sturgeon's considerable structural strength. The geometry of the retraction system for the main undercarriage legs is also illustrated here. In the T.T. Mk 2, the fuselage was deepened slightly in order to accommodate a crawlway for the observer, normally siuated amidships, to gain access to the nose station. The recess along the upper fuselage will carry the slide mechanism for the pilot's cockpit canopy.

Above: A close-up photograph taken in 1954 of the new nose fitted to the Sturgeon T.T. Mk 3 tugs. It was similar in general appearance to that of the original Mk 1 aircraft, but did not duplicate it. The odd black streak along the underside is a vestigial target-tug stripe: the width, angle and locations of these stripes were very precisely determined by the hierarchy, and airframe contours sometimes produced strange results.

alternative reconnaissance load was the installation of one F.24 and two F.52 cameras in the lower fuselage.

The Sturgeon T.T. Mk 2, developed, as we have seen, from the Mk 1 as a target tug, had a crew of two. It used the same wings and engines, but the Merlin 140s drove either de Havilland or Rotol six-bladed metal airscrews instead of the S. 1's wooden blades. The principal differences from the Mk 1 were the extended nose for the camera and camera operator in the aircraft's 'throw-off' shooting rôle which folded downwards for carrier stowage, the revolving, turret-like rear upper cupola from which towed targets could be observed and photographed, the target towing gear stowed internally in the bomb bay and a retractable power-driven Miles hydraulic winch. Stowing the drogue in the bottom of the fuselage avoided the drag of the arm and 'windmill' characteristic of some earlier target-towers.

From the outside the aircraft differed greatly at its front end, but little elsewhere. The winch gear was accommodated in the rear part of the centre section and took the space vacated by the removal of the downward-facing cameras, although the lower part of the fuselage had been enlarged to assist accessibility. The tailplane was the same as that on the bomber except that a ten-hundredweight steel cable was now stretched from the tips of the tailplane to the top of the rudder to prevent the 6,000-foot towing wire from fouling the structure; this cable was continued from the tailplane tips down to the fuselage. There was also an attachment in the tailwheel to prevent the tow cable from being entangled with the wheel when towing a winged target from a standing start.

The extended nose was constructed in the same orthodox form as the rest of the Sturgeon, namely stringers and frames covered by flush-riveted Alclad skinning. Transparent panels were fitted to the front and starboard side (for viewing both the ship firing its guns for practice and the shell bursts caused thereby), while a clear Perspex moulding was placed above the camera operator and formed part of the external shape of the nose.

The observer/wireless operator's station was to the rear to the cockpit, and he had a small rectangular window on each side of the fuselage above the level of the wing upper surface. There was no physical communication with the pilot, but these windows could be jettisoned as ditching exits for the aft compartment. The camera gun cupola position was placed on the fuselage upper deck to the rear of the observer/wireless operator's station and entry to the rear fuselage was via a hatch on the fuselage underside. The nose compartment could be entered through a hatch in the floor or via the bomb bay from the aft compartment and was only occupied when the photographic marking apparatus was to be used; the Mk 2's deeper fuselage allowed the second crewman to crawl underneath the pilot to the nose. A radio mast was fitted to the top of the fuselage approximately three feet abaft the pilot's canopy, and the only control in the pilot's cockpit associated with the machine's target-towing duties was an emergency cable cutter.

In both bomber and tug versions the fuel was carried internally in four Marston flexible wing tanks. In the Mk 2 there were 99 gallons in each of the outboard port and starboard wing tanks and 116 in each of the inboard wing tanks, making 430 gallons in all. The S. Mk 1's fuel capacity was two 95-gallon outboard and two 110-gallon tanks inboard, giving 410 gallons altogether, but for ferrying another 180 gallons could be made available by installing a tank in the bomb bay. In the Mk 2, the ferry range could be increased by fitting an auxiliary 60-gallon tank in the fuselage. The T.T. Mk 3 lost the long nose and all of the equipment needed to make deck landings such as powered wing folding and the arrester hook, although the wings could still be folded manually. In length this mark was 6 feet 9 inches shorter than the T.T. Mk 2.

Below: A Sturgeon Mk 2's port Merlin powerplant and contra-rotating propellers, showing their relatively short blades with their regulation yellow 'warning' tips; just in shot, to the left, is the nose folded down for stowage. The scoop-type intake beneath each engine is reminiscent of the arrangement in the Lancaster bomber, which of course also utilised the Merlin.

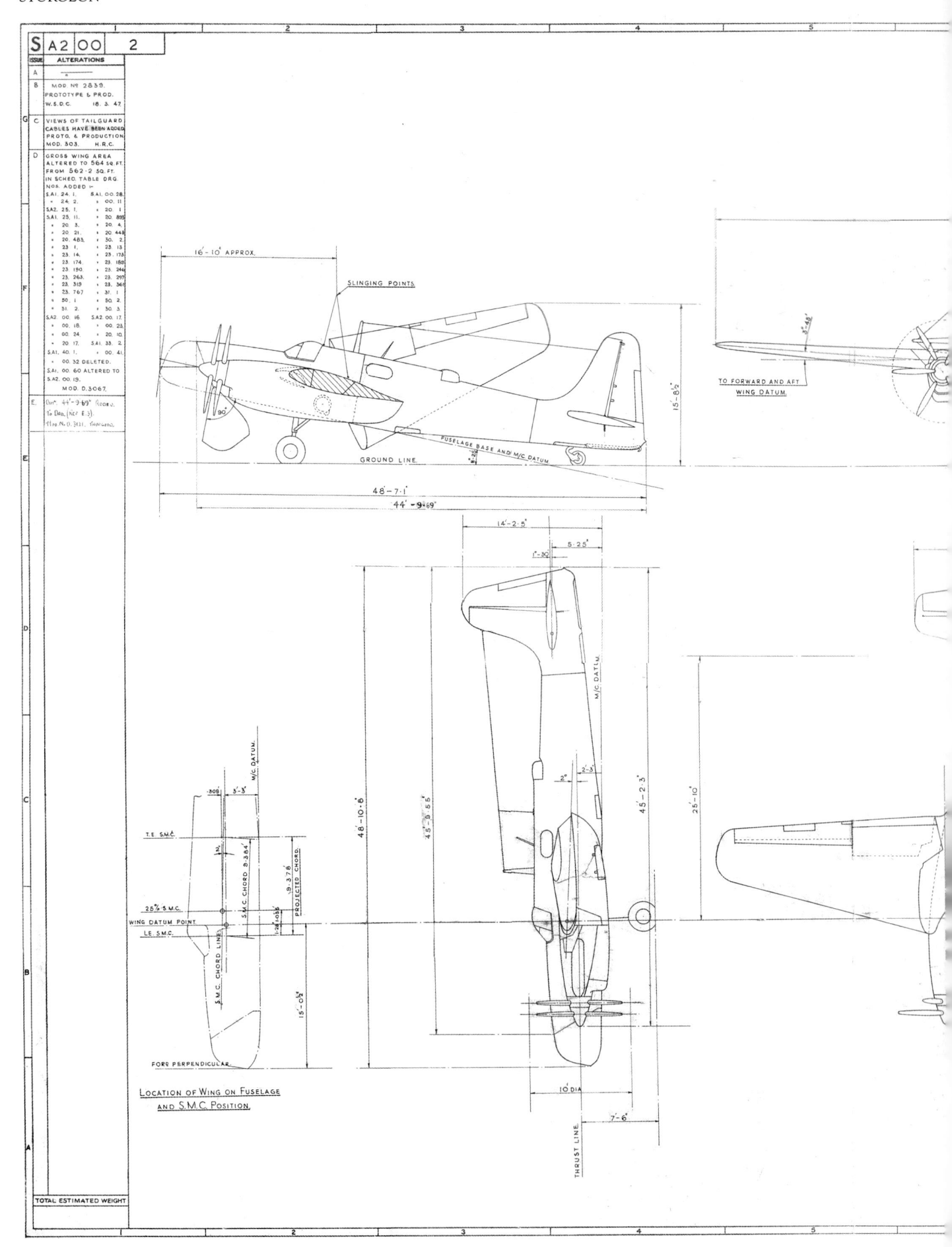

STURGEON

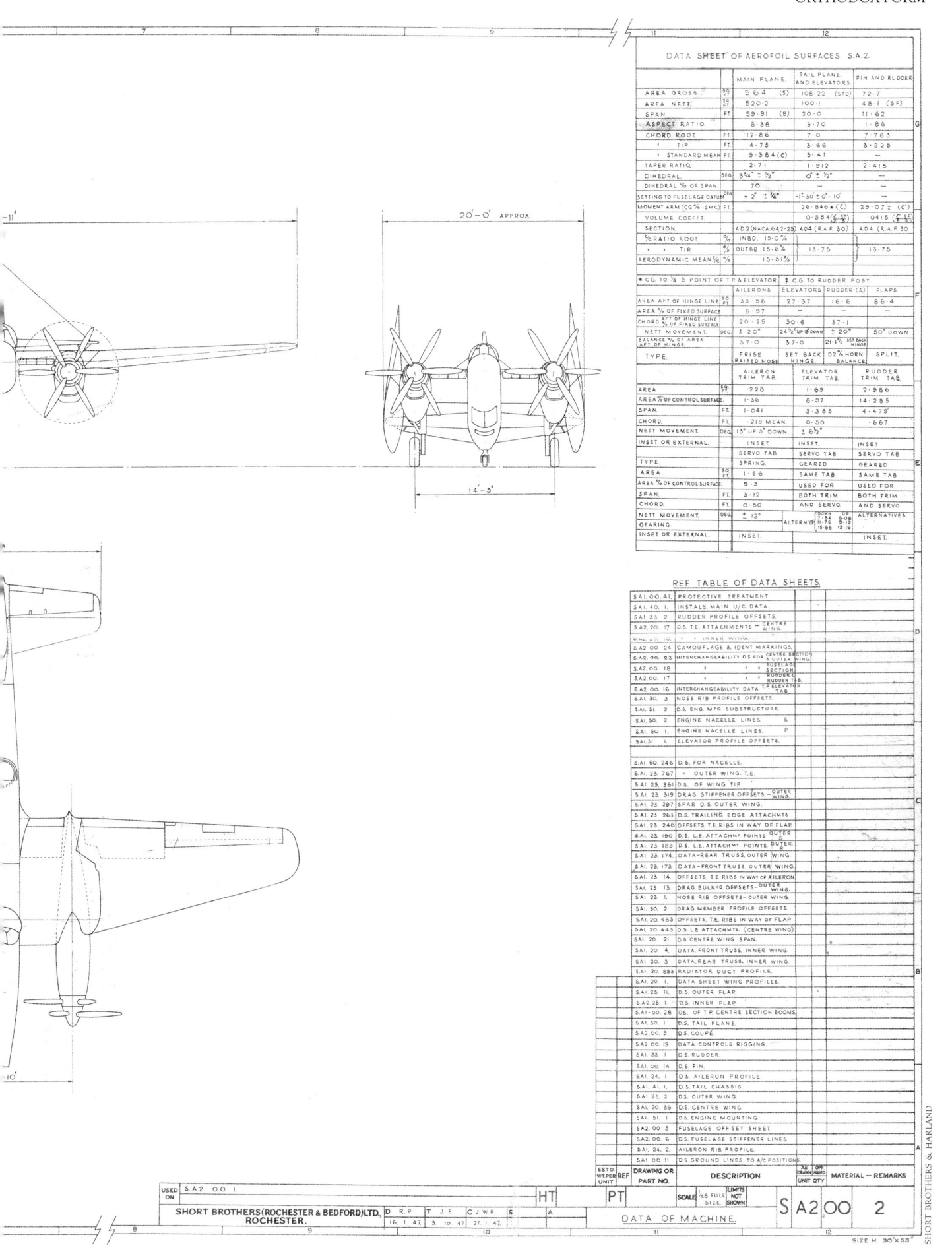

Above: A copy of the manufacturer's general-arrangement drawings for the Shorts S.A.2, otherwise known as the Sturgeon T.T. Mk 2. The specifications relate to VR363.

'A Gentlemanly Response'

The Sturgeon in the Air

DURING the 1940s and 1950s it was common for the reporters of the aviation magazines *Flight* and *The Aeroplane* to test-fly all manner of new aircraft, including some military types, and on 13 April 1951 (yes, a Friday!) G. Geoffrey Smith MBE from *Flight* and Derek D. Dempster of *The Aeroplane* were given the chance to assess Sturgeon T.T. Mk 2 TS486. Dempster's article was published in the 27 April 1951 issue of *The Aeroplane*, and extracts from it now follow.

The Sturgeon is a large aircraft, and the impression may therefore be gained that it is a little tricky to handle and quite a handful for deck operation. Not so, however; it is in fact what one might term a gentleman's aircraft, viceless in practically every way. I say practically viceless because the time taken to make a handling test is short and it would require more than one flight to discover any vicious tendencies. However, judging from the limited time I had in the cockpit, there is nothing that will baffle the average pilot.

The cockpit of the Sturgeon is delightfully roomy and cosily sunk in a well between the wings. Four flexible fuel tanks in pairs are placed in the centre section. Each pair feeds the appropriate engine and four fuel booster pumps are fitted, one in the bottom of each fuel tank. These are controlled by four switches on the cockpit's port sloping panel. Four electrically operated fuel gauges are situated at the bottom of the instrument panel with two fuel pressure warning lights below. The main hydraulic system operating the undercarriage, wing flaps, wing folding and radiator shutters is powered by two pumps driven by the port engine. All services in this system, with the exception of the radiator shutters, are controlled by push-buttons. The wing folding and undercarriage buttons are safely protected from inadvertent use by spring-loaded Perspex flaps, while the radiator shutters are controlled by switches on the instrument panel. Engine controls—throttles and rpm levers—are mounted on the port side of the cockpit, and the airscrew feathering push-buttons, which incorporate engine fire warning lights, at the top of the instrument panel.

Flying controls are quite normal, the control column being of the spade-grip pattern with incorporated brake lever. Dual-purpose tabs are fitted to the elevators and the rudder, acting as balance-tabs and as trimming-tabs controllable by handwheels pleasantly grouped below the throttle box. Operation of the ailerons is assisted by spring-tabs, the movement of which is determined by the air loads on the ailerons. Bias can be applied by a handwheel.

Starting up is fairly simple. Once the fuel cocks are opened and the engine primed with the required number of strokes, depending on the outside temperature, the ignition and the engine master starter switch may be turned on, and the Coffman starter fired. Taxiing is easy but the long nose obscures the forward view quite considerably so that it is necessary to swing the aircraft from side to side. Laterally the view is fairly good but to a certain extent obstructed by the engines and wings. Perhaps the most impressive thing about taxiing is the smoothness with which the Sturgeon rides, even over rough ground. The Messier oleo-pneumatic undercarriage, which is stressed to 16ft/sec vertical velocity, absorbs the worst shocks amazingly smoothly, even in a heavy landing. I was not entirely satisfied with the pneumatically operated brakes, however, as the brake lever was stiff and the brakes themselves rather sluggish to answer. Of course this may be a fault of the 12th production Sturgeon—the aircraft I flew—and may well be rectified.

For take-off, the drill is to set all three trimmers to neutral, the pitch control to give maximum rpm, and the flaps at take-off setting, not forgetting other checks such as the superchargers, harness and canopy. The latter, incidentally, is a moulded Perspex shell which can be opened and closed from outside by depressing the external release button just forward of the windscreen on the starboard side of the fuselage, and from the inside by means of a crank lever on the starboard side of the cockpit. It may be jettisoned if necessary by pulling a yellow-and-black striped lever mounted at the forward end of the cockpit coaming on the starboard side.

Vital actions completed, the aircraft is taxied forward to straighten the tail-wheel and the throttles opened against the brakes to give -2lb/sq.in. boost. Brakes released, the aircraft rolls away as power increases without the slightest tendency to swing whatsoever. The handling notes recommend that the Sturgeon should be flown off the ground at 85 knots (98mph), but it seems to take itself off without any help from the pilot. So smooth is the undercarriage suspension that I could barely tell the difference between rolling along the runway and flying. For a carrier take-off the throttles should be opened up against the brakes until the wheels begin to slip or the tail to lift. The brakes will hold the aircraft up to approximately 6lb/sq.in. boost, but if the deck is wet the wheels may slip before the engines reach this power.

Below: A photograph of TS486 taken during a flight over the coast of Antrim in 1950. TS486 served with 728 Squadron before being converted to T.T. Mk 3, first flying in this form on 2 December 1955.

Acceleration on take-off is fairly pronounced, and in the air, once the flaps and undercarriage are housed, the Sturgeon settles down to a steady climb. With a maximum climbing setting of +12lb/sq.in. boost, 2,850rpm and 140 knots (161mph), the Sturgeon's rate of ascent works out at about 2,450ft/min. at sea level, gradually falling off to 2,150ft/min. at 15,000ft. If the maximum rate of climb is not essential, more economical operation may be achieved by climbing at 140 knots using +9lb/sq.in. boost and 2,650rpm.

In the air the Sturgeon handles extraordinarily well and is easy to trim under all conditions of flight except at airspeeds of 70 knots (81mph) and below, with undercarriage and flaps down, power on. Changes in trim are slight when ancillaries are dropped. A nose-down change of trim occurs when the undercarriage is lowered and a nose-up tendency when the flaps go down. Radiator shutter operation gives little change of trim at the lower end of the speed scale, but the change becomes increasingly marked as the speed is increased. Radiator shutters open, the nose rises and vice versa when they are closed. When set to automatic control, the radiator shutters may open asymmetrically, causing considerable change of trim at the higher end of the speed scale. When I was flying there was a strong tendency to drop the port wing at speeds in excess of 210 knots (242mph).

All the control surfaces are effective and light, with the exception of the ailerons which, to my mind, are sluggish. At speeds at or near the stall they lose much of their effectiveness although there is ample control available. The trimmers are effective throughout the speed range, especially the rudder trimmer which is positive and will hold the aeroplane on a steady course with one engine out, even at fairly low speeds. Power response to throttle movement is slow, and at low power settings a large movement is required for small changes in power. Level speeds at maximum power for climb and emergency cruising at an all-up weight of about 20,000lb work out at about 247 knots (284mph) at sea level, and at maximum continuous cruising power, 230 knots (265mph). Stalling the Sturgeon is a gentle pastime, and at an all-up-weight of 20,000lb with undercarriage and flaps housed, power off, this stall occurs at 80 knots (92mph). With all the paraphernalia lowered and the engines on, the aeroplane stalls at 65 knots (75mph).

Warning of the stall's approach under the first conditions is given by slight buffeting, starting some six or seven knots (7 or 8mph) above and increasing down to the stall. At the stall, the nose falls away gently with little tendency to drop either wing. If a wing does drop it usually appears to be the port one. With the undercarriage and flaps down, the buffeting occurs some four to five knots (4.5 to 6mph) before the stall, which is characterised by a fairly marked aileron snatch just before the stall. When the aircraft does stall at 75 knots (86mph), the wing drops gently. Under the same conditions, but with power on, the speed may be reduced to as low as 65 knots (75mph) provided that the weight does not exceed 20,000lb, the maximum landing weight, but the resulting stall is not so gentle. The port wing drops suddenly, causing the aircraft to turn through about 50°. Release of pressure on the control column insures immediate recovery.

Manoeuvrability in general is good for an aircraft designed for such steady work. I had a gnawing desire to try some aerobatics during my flight in it, but unfortunately this machine is not stressed for such frivolities. I was apprehensive about the folding wings but these, I was assured later, will only fold on the ground when the weight of the aircraft is solidly planted on the undercarriage. A further safety device ensures that folding is impossible in the air. Before taking off one or two members of Short Brothers and Harland Ltd apologised in advance for the excessive noise in the cockpit, but I found it, by comparison with other aircraft I have flown, comparatively quiet, especially when taking into consideration the fact that the engines are only a few feet away. They also warned me about poor forward visibility in rain, but a healthy rainstorm I purposely flew through showed that it was not half as bad as I had anticipated.

For the final approach and landing I received a gentlemanly response from the Sturgeon, which should be flown in on the approach at 95 knots (109mph) with undercarriage and flaps down, and a power setting of about −4lb/sq.in. boost, crossing the boundary at 85 knots (98mph) or just under. Three-point landings are easy provided power is maintained right up to the touch-down, but if the throttles are closed too early, the elevator control is such that it is difficult to get the tail down. Deck landings should be made off an approach starting at 85 knots (98mph) with fully fine pitch and 2lb/sq.in. boost, diminishing after the final turn-in to 80 knots (92mph) at +1lb/sq.in. boost. The arrester hook is lowered by raising a hook-shaped handle on the starboard side of the cockpit, but cannot be raised except manually. When the hook is down, an indicator light just above the hook control lights up.

One point I have not mentioned is that the Zapp wing flaps have three positions only: 'Up', 'Take-Off' and 'Down'. They cannot be stopped intermediately. As previously stated, they are operated in the same way as the undercarriage and wing-spreading control—by push-buttons mounted on a box below the compass on the port side of the cockpit. After landing and parking, the engines should be idled at 1,200rpm for thirty seconds to allow even cooling. They are stopped by pressing and holding in the two slow-running cut-out buttons to the left and below the pilot's seat.

Below: Another photograph of TS486, which, like the previous picture, was taken during a flight over the coast of Northern Ireland in 1950. This aircraft was the production Sturgeon taken on a test flight by Derek Dempster on 13 April 1951.

No further production of the type is contemplated and the jigs are being taken down. I count myself fortunate, therefore, that I was able to try one out before they were all commissioned.

Captain Eric Brown CBE DSC AFC, the renowned test pilot, flew the Sturgeon some four years earlier, when the prototype, RK787, was dispatched to the Royal Aircraft Establishment at Farnborough in April 1947 for arresting proofing and deck-landing assessment. It 'sailed through the former with no hitches,' he recalls. For the latter assessment,

> ... the aircraft was at an all-up weight of 18,500 pounds with the centre of gravity on the forward limit. The reason for this CG position was to represent a similar handling condition to that of the later long-nosed production Sturgeon II at normal loading and CG.
>
> The Sturgeon I was a purposeful, sturdy looking aeroplane and this impression of robustness had certainly been confirmed in the faultless way it went through its arresting proofing trials. However, in getting into the cockpit I was disappointed at the view provided, because the windscreen was not high enough on the sloping nose, and the overhang shields round the instrument panel encroached much too high on the windscreen side-panels.
>
> The two 1,660hp Merlin 140S engines started with their usual efficiency, and there was a great blur created by the airscrew discs just ahead of the nose. During taxying the aircraft had a slight tendency to weathercock in a crosswind, but in spite of the brakes not being very powerful, there was no real problem in steering the Sturgeon on the ground.
>
> For a carrier type of take-off the brakes held the aircraft up to plus 7 pounds boost before they started to slip, but then full power could be applied because of the lack of swing due to the contra-props. Using 'Take-Off' flap the unstick distance in the three-point attitude was very short with plus 20 pounds boost.
>
> The change of trim on raising the undercarriage was negligible, and that on raising the flaps only slightly nose down. The best setting of the radiator flaps for take-off seemed to be one-quarter open, and all trims were neutral. The rate of climb was good, but the cockpit was noisy and very hot. In normal cruising flight the aircraft exhibited marginally positive stick free stability, and that was about ideal for its strike/reconnaissance rôle. Harmony of control was good, and all controls were effective in response.
>
> The stalling characteristics of a naval aircraft are particularly important in view of its low margin of speed above the stall on a deck-landing approach. The essentials are ample pre-stall warning and lack of a severe wing drop at the actual stall. The Sturgeon had sufficient pre-stall buffeting and a gentle fore-and-aft oscillation before the nose dropped away squarely at 80 knots all-up, and 75 knots with undercarriage and flaps down. In fact the all-down stall was difficult to produce, requiring full backward elevator trim and stick movement to produce it. The application of engine power did not alter the stalling characteristics markedly, except that if the stall was approached very gently it was possible to get through the fore-and-aft pitching and produce a starboard wing drop with a slight snatch of the stick to starboard.
>
> The crunch test was of course the simulated deck landing. The undercarriage was lowered at 125 knots and had little effect on trim, whilst lowering the flaps to the 'Take-Off' position at 100 knots gave a slight nose-up change of trim, and then to the 'Down' position at 90 knots a stronger nose-down change. Opening the radiator flaps fully gave a nose-up pitch to ease the overall nose-down trim effect.
>
> The best landing speed was 75 knots at 0 boost, but at that speed all the controls suffered in effectiveness and particularly the ailerons, which became spongy in feel although the elevators and rudder remained light. However, longitudinal stick fix stability was excellent, and this, combined with a throttle quadrant that gave adequate coarseness of engine control, enabled a well-controlled approach path to be maintained. A hard pull back on the stick was required at the last moment to effect a three-point touchdown. Even if a three-pointer was not achieved, the undercarriage was so soft that no bounce was likely. There was no swing after landing, and although the brakes were not very powerful the landing run was exceptionally short.

The whole landing process with the Sturgeon reminded one vividly of the Barracuda, which was a very good deck-landing aircraft if little else. The view ahead was good on the approach in the Sturgeon, but it was drastically affected by rain, although the rear two-thirds of the curved side screens remained clear enough to enable safe deck landings to be made. The next step was to try an asymmetric deck-landing approach, but this proved not to be feasible because the lateral control became too heavy and spongy to bring the speed down to acceptable limits for such an operation.

The Sturgeon was really the last attempt with a twin piston-engine aeroplane to solve the single-engine deck-landing problem, for the axial-flow jet engine arrived on the scene and its slim shape and lack of airscrew allowed the two engines to be housed close together and so the problem solved itself with such a layout. Nevertheless, I remember it as an interesting attempt to solve a difficult problem, and it just might have succeeded with more development time.

Above: The first Sturgeon, RK747, which Captain Brown flew for arresting proofing and deck-landing assessment trials at RAE Farnborough. There were some disappointments, as he explains in the accompanying text. In this photograph, the aircraft's port Merlin has been shut down and the propellers feathered.

Target Matters

The Sturgeon as a Fleet Requirements Aircraft

DURING World War II the requirement for specialist target-towing aircraft was a relatively minor priority, and, as a result, the aircraft chosen for such work tended to be types which had proved unsuitable for operational duties, or were obsolescent, or were in ready supply and could be easily converted, such as the Miles Master and Martinet. With the cessation of hostilities it became apparent that the Royal Navy would need a high-performance target-tower capable of being operated from an aircraft carrier. Given such facilities, the Navy could then maintain a high standard of gunnery, not only ship-to-air but also air-to-air, throughout the whole of a long cruise and far beyond the range of shore-based target towing aircraft. Thus, for a comparatively small cost, the fleets could be kept to a higher war standard than might otherwise be possible, and it was this objective that brought the Sturgeon target tug into being.

The need for a representative high-performance 'enemy' aircraft thus became of great importance, which meant that some of the Service's best aircraft might have to be diverted from front-line squadrons to carry out this work. Had the war continued, it is likely that the Sturgeon would have been used in the bomber rôle for which it was originally designed, but its robust construction and good turn of speed made the type well suited for conversion into a target-tug. During the war ships at sea could only get anti-aircraft gunnery practice while in the close vicinity of a naval air station equipped with aircraft from a fleet requirements unit; for example, a convoy taking the six-week journey from England to the Cape would get firing practice perhaps only for a few hours in the approaches to Bathurst (Sierra Leone). If the Fleet were on a long cruise away from land, this arrangement

Left: A view of the long nose that distinguished the Mk 2 from other Sturgeons— necessary because the camera equipment had not only to 'see' forward but also to the starboard beam, in order to record the results of 'throw-off' gunnery.

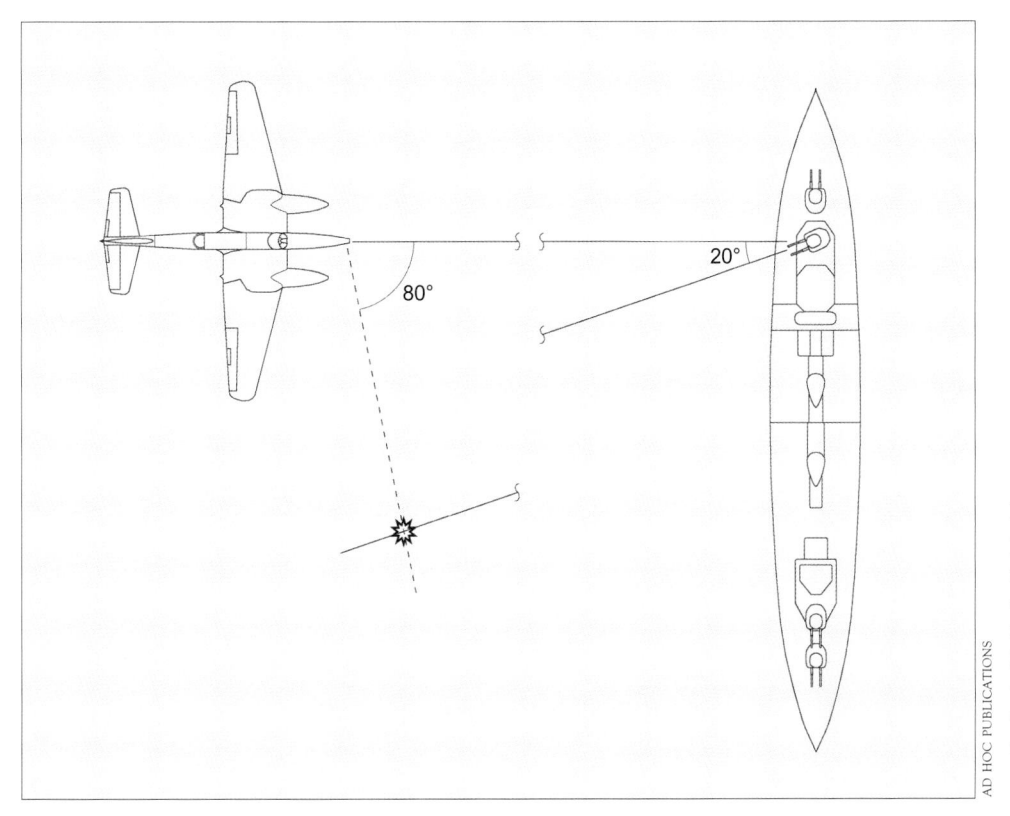

Left: A diagram to illustrate the principles of 'throw-off' gunnery. Radar-directed gunfire rendered the technique redundant shortly after the Sturgeon entered service, and the aircraft's duties thereafter were confined largely to target-towing and radar calibration.

meant there were substantial periods when such training just could not be carried out, but embarking Sturgeons on board carriers would mean that gunnery practice could be laid on throughout a cruise. However, before the type was available in numbers the Navy replaced 'throw-off' target practice with radar gunlaying, and, as a result, very few Sturgeons ever went to sea—and probably none operationally.

To understand better the requirements issued covering the Sturgeon target-tug (and laid down in Specification Q.1/46, alluded to earlier), it is necessary to appreciate that in aircraft gunnery practice the gun barrels were offset 20 degrees from the sight. The gunners aimed at the Sturgeon and would fire live shells, but the barrels were pointing 20 degrees to port and so the bursts all exploded at a predetermined distance to the side of the aircraft. This was known as 'throw-off' gunnery, and the Vinten measuring camera carried in the Sturgeon assessed the accuracy of the firing by photographing, simultaneously, both the ship and the shell bursts some 80 degrees on the side. In its original bomber form, the Sturgeon would have been unable to perform this photography because the engines would have been in the way, masking the shell bursts. Therefore, the camera had to be mounted ahead of the engines to cover the 80-degree angle, and indeed to allow this angle to be swivelled back another 20–30 degrees—i.e., slightly backwards—to ensure that errors in aim were seen by the camera without the aircraft's structure blocking the view. This is why the Sturgeon T.T. Mk 2 had its long nose, but the five-foot extension to the fuselage in this modification put the aircraft's overall length beyond the specified maximum of 45 feet (which in turn was fixed by the length of aircraft carrier lifts). Shorts' novel way of solving this problem was to make the front fuselage fold downwards, to give a folded length of 44 feet 9.4 inches. It was for filming 'throw-off' gunfire that the observer had to move forward to work the camera. When the Sturgeon was being used as a target-tower (Q.1/46 called for the aeroplane to do either one or the other operation, but not both at once), the observer/winch operator did not have to make his way to the forward compartment and so the winch could be placed in the intercommunicating tunnel space. This passage could also hold the special 60-gallon ferry fuel tank which was removed when the aircraft was needed for 'tugging' duties.

Pulling, Not Pushing

The Sturgeon in Squadron Service

THE Sturgeon S. Mk 1 bomber, and the later S.B.3 anti-submarine variant discussed above (see pages 36–43), were flown only in prototype form and so never reached a service unit. The T.T Mk 2s and 3s that did join the Royal Navy all served as a target-tugs and so the units they operated with were second-line and concerned with training and trials.

In 1951 703 Naval Air Squadron was the Royal Navy's Service Trials Unit, based at RNAS Ford. It flew a small number of Sturgeon T.T. Mk 2s between April and August 1951. The Commanding Officer at the time was Lieutenant-Commander J. M. Glaser DSC. TS477 was coded '004/FD' and TS483 '003/FD', the letters signifying their Ford base. TS475 also flew briefly with 703 in October and November 1949 as '089'.

771 Squadron also operated as a fleet requirements unit and the fixed-wing element of this unit had received its first Sturgeon T.T. Mk 2s in September 1950 while based at Lee-on-Solent under the command of Lieutenant-Commander J. G. Baldwin DSC. On 18 December Baldwin was succeeded as CO by Lieutenant-Commander J. A. Welply, and then by Lieutenant-Commander M. W. Rudolf DSC on 5 May 1952. The Sturgeon left 771 in November 1952, just two months after the Squadron had moved its headquarters to Ford as the Southern Fleet Requirements Unit. One example on 771's strength was TS491, which to begin with bore the code '093/FD' but was later seen as '586/FD'. At least four other Sturgeons joined at some time during the commission, including TS482 ('592/FD'), TS484 ('590/FD') and TS490 ('587/FD').

Lieutenant-Commander Peter Hiles served with 703 Squadron in the early 1950s and remembers that, because of the considerable intervals that elapsed between the availability of aircraft and equipment that were to be subjected to official trials, much of the flying undertaken by him and his Squadron colleagues was spent 'stooging' for ships and shore stations, mostly rather boringly backwards and forwards so that radars could be calibrated and gunners exercised. The trials themselves, moreover, would be conducted only after Farnborough or Boscombe Down had completed theirs. With a hint of justified indignation, he recalls that 703 were required to test their subject aircraft to give an appreciation of how 'ordinary pilots' (!) might cope behind the controls. 'Oh, how we resented that!' he remarks. 'Of *course* we could!'

On 18 April 1951 two Sturgeons, TS482 and TS484, arrived at RNAS Ford for a brief assignation with 703 Squadron; meanwhile the trials carrier, HMS *Illustrious*, was preparing to steam up the Channel towards a rendezvous with the aircraft, though the ship would be in the vicinity of the Sussex coast only on 30 April and 1 May. The intervening period was spent getting used to the aircraft, and of course conducting the inevitable Aerodrome Dummy Deck Landings. However, as Lieutenant-Commander Hiles explains,

The real purpose of the exercise, undertaken by Jimmy Duncan (seconded to 703 from Boscombe) and me in TS482, was to pull the arrester wires of the carrier with a heavier than usual aircraft, with a view to preparing the systems for future front-line aircraft, rather than to assess the deck-landing performance of the Sturgeon itself; I think it had already been decided that the aircraft would not be used in a carrier-borne rôle. We were not concerned with the aircraft's landing qualities as such, and there was certainly no question of carrying out single-engine landings. The Sturgeon was pretty nimble in flight, however, and its single-engine performance was extremely good. There was very little 'pull', but the potential difficulty was that, on approach to the carrier, the landing speed with one engine 'out' would have been insufficient to have enabled the aircraft, in the event of second attempt being called for, to gain power, climb away and 'go round again'. Something that I was quite unused to, however, was the excellent view forward on the approach! I note that on 1 May I made six landings in a forty-minute sortie from Ford, this forty minutes having to include re-spotting the aircraft on deck for each take-off.

Lieutenant-Commander Hiles also recalls an occasion when he formated with Jimmy Duncan when the latter was flying one of the Armstrong Whitworth A.W.52 'Flying Wings'—a rare experience and, of course, quite another story!

The primary operator of the Short Sturgeon target-tug was 728 Naval Air Squadron, and it was also the only unit to fly both the T.T. Mk 2 and the T.T Mk 3 'on active duty'. This squadron was a Fleet Requirements Unit and was based at Hal Far in Malta from May 1946 until it disbanded at the end of May 1967. The primary rôle of an FRU is to train personnel on board Royal Navy warships in defensive techniques and procedures concerning air attack—a task of paramount importance. During the period covered by the Sturgeon, FRUs would usually fly combat aircraft that had just left the front line but which were ideal for

Below: T.T. Mk 2 TS496, in sparkling condition, parked during a visit to the Naval Fighter School at RNAS Culdrose in 1952 or 1953 while serving with 771 Squadron at Ford.

STURGEON

making mock attacks on warships to allow radar and gun operators to track them. To illustrate this, during the time that 728 had Sturgeons on strength it also flew, for example, Supermarine Seafires, de Havilland Mosquitos and Sea Hornets, and de Havilland Sea Vampire jets. The first Sturgeon T.T. Mk 2s arrived in August 1951 and began to replace Mosquito T.T. Mk 39 tugs. The Mk 2 served with 728 until January 1956 as the surviving examples were converted to Mk 3s, the latter having been 'introduced' in July 1954.

No 728's Commanding Officers during the Sturgeon period were Lieutenant-Commander H. A. Monk DSM, who was in charge when the type arrived, Lieutenant-Commander P. C. S. Bagley from 6 February 1952, Lieutenant-Commander A. D. Corkhill DSC from 1 January 1954, Lieutenant-Commander B. Bevans from 26 January 1955, and Lieutenant-Commander R. C. B. Trelawney, who took over on 27 May 1957 and who was still with the unit when the Sturgeon was withdrawn. 728 was based at Hal Far to provide training and practice facilities for the Royal Navy's Mediterranean Fleet, but during the Sturgeon's career it was also increasingly called upon by the British Army and the RAF Regiment (to train the crews of their anti-aircraft batteries), and sometimes by the United States Navy.

Top: 771 Squadron's TS496 again at Culdrose, here running up its Merlins. Above: TS482 whilst serving with 771 Squadron at RNAS Lee-on-Solent in 1951. This was the aircraft that, on loan to 703 Squadron at nearby RNAS Ford, Lieutenant-Commander Peter Hiles flew on arresting trials on board HMS *Illustrious* that year—as he himself recalls on pages 62–63. The fuselage call-sign is, rather unusually, positioned forward of the yellow band.

Commander Andy Phillip was, as a 'two-and-a-half', Lieutenant-Commander (Operations) at RNAS Hal Far (HMS *Falcon*) from April 1956 to August 1958—a tour which, of course, took in the Suez Crisis—and is thus ideally qualified to describe the context in which 728 Squadron undertook its duties. It was Lieutenant-Commander (Ops)'s task, he recalls, to liaise with the fleet carriers deployed to the Mediterranean; to ensure that the Air Station's activities were co-ordinated with those of the Fleet and that the engineering and workshop facilities at Kalafrana were available to it; and to organise generally. Thus he himself did quite a bit of flying, using the S-51 Dragonfly helicopter for liaison work with and between carriers and the Sea Devons and Expeditors based at Hal Far in a communications capacity—to and from Gibraltar and Cyprus, or perhaps taking the C-in-C to Rome or wherever he was required to be. As Lieutenant-Commander (Ops) he had an intimate knowledge of fleet movements and also their requirements and would ensure, in concert with the COs, that the Station's assets were deployed on time, and to the correct ranges, whenever they were called upon. But, he remembers, 'One of my main tasks, as far as I could see it, was to try to keep the carriers out of trouble in a diplomatic sense—appraising the carrier commanders of the potential trouble spots and advising generally. I recall one occasion, for example, when a carrier squadron conducted some bombing practice on a French range without proper permission!'

He continues:

We also had VP-23, a large squadron of US P2V-7 Neptunes (handy for a number of 'extracurricular' reasons!), on base for a period and of course the carrier squadrons would disembark to Hal Far when the ships were visiting Grand Harbour. The Air Station could get extremely busy at times—on one occasion there were nine squadrons in residence, most of them temporarily of course—and thus successful co-ordination was another of my priorities.

On my visits to Gib I would meet the carriers' Commanders (Ops), or occasionally their Commanders (Air), in order to discuss the ships' schedules—in particular their range requirements (for example, Filfla Rock for rocketing and bombing), their date of departure from Gibraltar and their estimated time of arrival off Malta—and on return to Hal Far would get down to planning the Station's programme in detail. There were many ranges in and around Malta. All were well used, and apart from Filfla there were air-to-air ranges for drogue- and target-towing and two anti-submarine ranges for torpedo and mine dropping, some of these areas overlapping. In addition, there were two ranges for large-ship

Below: One of the classic studies of a Sturgeon is this one, taken with Mount Etna as a background in 1952 or 1953. Several frames were captured on the sortie; another appears on pages 70–71. They were shot by 728 Squadron's Senior Observer and Hal Far's Photographic Officer, Lieutenant (now Commander) Gordon Roberts, who relates some of his experiences in this book.

firings against towed surface targets, while the Royal Malta Artillery and the RAF Regiment would also request targets for their AA guns. Hence the use of the ranges had to be very carefully co-ordinated so that all the varying requirements could be met. NATO range facilities, however, were organised through the various Operational Area Commanders, thereby enabling carriers that were in transit to continue training right through the Mediterranean without stopping in Maltese waters.

Requests for target-towing by the Sturgeons would be relayed to Lascaris, the communications headquarters on Malta, where I attended Weekly Planning meetings to help organise the programme and arrange priority tasking; the 728 Squadron CO would also be at these meetings if his aircraft were being called upon. My job was to make sure that everybody knew what was taking place on the ranges and what was required of Hal Far, for example, where the ships that were calling on our services were operating, and when. Other activities, such as AI interceptions, might also be taking place in a particular area, and so it was necessary to know the details of these too—and not only the Navy but also the RAF and sometimes the Army would require the use of the ranges. Air-to-air firing, for example, required quite a lot of airspace. Things got very hectic when the Suez operation was building up—there was a great deal of coming and going as several carriers were involved. The Sturgeons were detached to Cyprus for a period, I recall, possibly at about this time.

Lieutenant-Commander 'Cue' Cureton served with 728 from May 1957 until December 1959 and remembered that the exercises carried out by the Sturgeon were many and varied. There were the usual Squadron formation and war strikes, but specific to the aircraft itself were the following:

1. Gunnery tracking: Both non-firing and off-shoot live firing. 20mm, Bofors and 4.5-inch guns.
2. Towing: Sleeves, banner and 32-foot winged targets. This was for ships of the Fleet and for the various forts and other establishments. There was also fighter interception with live ammunition.
3. Radio trials: At long range for W/T and voice radio.

He also recalled that towing for the US Sixth Fleet was especially interesting—and that each of these sorties was of quite short duration. The Royal Navy's Mediterranean Fleet used only one gun station at a run (probably for reasons of economy), whereas ships of the US Navy tended not to waste time and every gun station, from 0.5in machine guns to 4in turrets, took part at the same time: 'We ran out of sleeves every time,' he says, 'and reeled in very short lengths of wire!'

Below: 728 Squadron's T.T.2 TS476 at Hal Far Air Show on 28 August 1954. Hawker Sea Hawk fighter WM918, on charge to the Hal Far AHU at the time, stands alongside, with a Lockheed Neptune maritime patrol aircraft of VP-21 beyond. The Sturgeon here later bore the side number '593' and is reported as being converted to Mk 3 standard during 1956.

Above: T.T.2 TS486, its flaps dropped to the maximum of 50 degrees, makes its landing approach. On a return from a towing sortie using a winged target, the landing was always a co-operative effort involving the Sturgeon aircrew and a ground controller, keeping in touch by R/T, the objective being a safe recovery of the target so that it could be used in further sorties. The target, having been reeled in to some 300 feet, was released when it touched the runway by the aircrewman winch operator, who, 'feeling' the impact, would cut the tow with bolt-cutters.

Lieutenant Peter Dallosso joined 728 Squadron at HMS *Falcon* in June 1954 under Lieutenant-Commander A. D. Corkhill, and as well as flying Sturgeons and the other types based there he also undertook the duties of Squadron Staff Officer. He amassed some 93 hours in Sturgeons of both marks, carrying out 'tugging' with 32-foot winged targets (eighteen sorties) and with sleeves for air-to-air firing; gunnery radar/tracking; photographic target marking; and dummy strikes on both the Mediterranean and the US Sixth Fleets. The sheer size of the Royal Navy's presence in the Mediterranean is difficult to comprehend these days. 'HMS *Cumberland*, the gunnery trials ships, featured a lot,' he recalls, 'and we also worked with the aircraft carrier *Centaur*, the cruiser *Gambia*, the Third Destroyer Squadron (*Daring*, etc.), the Fifth Frigate Squadron and many submarines—as well as with the RNVR air squadrons on their summer cruise. It was an enormous fleet in those days.'

Flying the Sturgeon was straightforward enough, he says, although starting the engines was sometimes difficult and, being a tail-wheeled aircraft, care had to be taken in crosswinds when taking off or landing. One or two incidents remain etched in his memory:

> The winged target was designed in such a way that, if the cable broke in flight, the target itself would pitch down smartly and dive into the sea. However, on one occasion *Cumberland* shot the tail off one of my winged target tows and we brought back merely the nose and wings. On another occasion we were towing air-to-air drogues for 806 Squadron's Sea Hawks, but we lost our tow when the cable was shot away. We were left with only two-thirds of our towing wire—though fortunately we had 6,000 feet of cable deployed at the time!

Between February and March 1954 Lieutenant Harry Hands underwent a heavy twin conversion course at RNAS St Davids in Pembrokeshire, where he enjoyed twenty-five hours on the Mosquito T.III, and on 17 March 1954 joined 728 Squadron at Hal Far, whose fleet requirements aircraft at the time comprised Sea Hornet Mk 20s, Vampires, Expeditors, Meteor T.7s and Sturgeons. The last were

Above: A forlorn TS484, which crashed at Hal Far in November 1953 after an undercarriage leg struck a wall on landing. The pilot, Lieutenant Sloane, was unhurt—although, as can be seen from the state of the cockpit canopy, he was indeed fortunate—and the aircraft was eventually repaired and returned to service. Several of 728's long-nose Sturgeons carried the Squadron crest on the port side forward, as depicted here. The names visible further aft record this particular aircraft's ground-crewmen— 'Pilot [sic] Mate L.A. Lucas' and 'Fitter N.A. Bevan'.

T.T.2s, though in time all the aircraft were converted to T.T.3 short-nose versions. He recalls:

> I served under two COs during my time at Hal Far, Lieutenant-Commander A. D. Corkhill and Lieutenant-Commander B. Bevans, and the Senior Pilot was Lieutenant-Commander N. L. Sharrock. Squadron members included Lieutenant-Commander C. W. G. Drake, Lieutenants Lewis, Bradley, Willcox, Mellor, Roncoroni, Walman, Jenne, Pickthall, Dallosso, Fyfe and O'Connell, Sub-Lieutenant Hick and Messrs Stimpson and Warren; and among our crewmen were CPOs Homer and Collyer, Tels Webb, Morley and Mann and Mr McIntyre. I flew some 160 hours on Sturgeons, our principal tasks being sleeve towing for the Army, winged target towing, air-to-air drogue towing, photographic marking, radar calibration and throw-off target practice. We worked a good deal with the destroyers and cruisers of the Mediterranean Fleet.
>
> The Sturgeon was a reasonably straightforward from the pilot's point of view, although occasionally amusement was caused when start-up instead became fire practice owing to the proximity of the fire extinguisher buttons in the cockpit to those for the engine start! The twin contra-rotating propellers, close in to the fuselage, certainly enhanced single-engine flying, and the aircraft's general performance improved greatly when the long nose of the T.T.2 was removed in the conversion process, giving the aircraft something of the appearance of a Merlin-powered Beaufighter. The aircraft was essentially reliable in my experience, although I did suffer a couple of main undercarriage problems, a tailwheel problem and one engine failure. The story was that each Sturgeon had been hand-built at a cost of £500,000 per aircraft—a considerable sum for those days.
>
> Flying techniques involving targets called for some extra attention. For take-off, the aircraft was run up to full power with the brakes on, the stick was pulled well back and then the brakes were released and we dragged the target into the air to about 1,000 feet, where it more or less fell into straight and level. This technique was designed so as to guarantee the shortest possible take-off run for the target, which was, as it were, 'snatched' into the air. Landing entailed making a high and slow approach, a matelot having already been positioned alongside the runway. The landing itself was steep and well up the runway, allowing the target to be released just as it crossed the threshold. The target would then land, usually veering off the runway proper as it slowed, but generally with very little damage and still airworthy. Ships' gunners were supposed to lay off when shooting, but of course there was always someone on board with a juvenile streak who thought it fun to try to plant some holes in the wrong place. Fortunately, we were not required to land damaged targets back at Hal Far, and these incidents gave rise to the oft-heard comment over the aircrew R/T, 'I'm glad I'm pulling this thing and not pushing it.'

A few little memories. On 2 April 1954, having completed Fam I and Fam II on a Sturgeon, I was briefed to fly T.T.2 TS495 (call-sign '595') in Exercise 'Shield One', which involved 'strikes' on Tunisian and Sicilian airfields. I pointed out that I had not completed Fam III, so it was suggested that I take my copy of the Pilot's Notes along and do it while returning from the sortie. However, on pulling up from a low pass over Marsala airfield I noticed that the port engine was losing a lot of oil and that the oil pressure was very low. I feathered the engine and called up the leader, to be told that there was no way that I was going to land in Sicily otherwise we would never get the aircraft back. 'Study your Pilot's Notes,' I was told, 'and prepare for a single-engine landing at Hal Far.' There seemed to be an awful lot of sea between Sicily and Malta! Nevertheless, the single-engine approach and landing was carried out successfully, and I must say that I was delighted with the aircraft's handling with only one Merlin functioning—and with getting Fam III and IV in my logbook!

On 20 April 1955, returning in Sturgeon TS493 ('586') from Operation 'Stainless', I was unable to lower my tailwheel. The main undercarriage was locked down, and on telling the Tower that I would be carrying out a 'wheelie' and keep the tail off the runway for as long as possible so as to minimise the damage, I was ordered to perform the 'wheelie' but to co-ordinate my brakes and throttle and come to a stop with the tail in the air, holding the aircraft on throttle alone, whereupon a trestle would be placed under the tail and no damage at all would be incurred! I made a couple of dummy runs and then landed, the groundcrew following the aircraft in their transport. As I stopped, they leapt out and got the trestle into position. No damage! Excellent—Sturgeons were enormously expensive to repair. I should point out that the Sturgeon lifted its tail on engine run-up quite easily unless the stick was held well back, but this particular landing was a little hairy—rather like trying to land a see-saw!

One fine day one of our Sturgeons was carrying out a normal approach for landing when we were amazed to see a winged target flying behind it. The aircraft touched down at the beginning of the runway as the target landed on a farmhouse, causing much consternation and huge claims for damages citing broken legs etc. (most of which were pure fiction). On another occasion—a few days later, in fact—a Sturgeon made a normal take-off from the opposite end of the same runway, keeping low after departure in order to build up the airspeed. The winged target being towed was dragged through the self-same farmhouse! Unsurprisingly, its occupants were not amused. The pilot involved shall be nameless, but it wasn't me!

Commander Gordon C. Roberts OBE completed the Officers' Long Photographic Course at RNAS Ford and the Joint Services Photographic Interpreters' Course at Nuneham Courtenay, Oxfordshire, during 1950–51 and in April 1951, as a Lieutenant (O) RN, was given a dual appointment to RNAS Hal Far as the

Overleaf: Another of the stunning photographs taken by Commander Gordon Roberts during the Etna fly-by. 728 Squadron's Sturgeons did not invariably have their call-signs repeated on the nose of the aircraft, as can be seen, and notice also the 'Cut here' markings around the observer's glazing and abaft the dorsal cupola, to facilitate the rescue of crew members in the event of an emergency.

Below: Mk 2 TS285 landing at RNAS Hal Far. In this instance the nose of the aircraft does bear a reduced version of the call-sign, together with a list of the crew names and a cartoon which appears to involve a character and a bottle of champagne but has so far eluded positive identification; perhaps it recalls a rather good evening at one of the local Maltese hostelries. The tail letters, common to most 728 Squadron Sturgeons for most of the time, require no explanation.

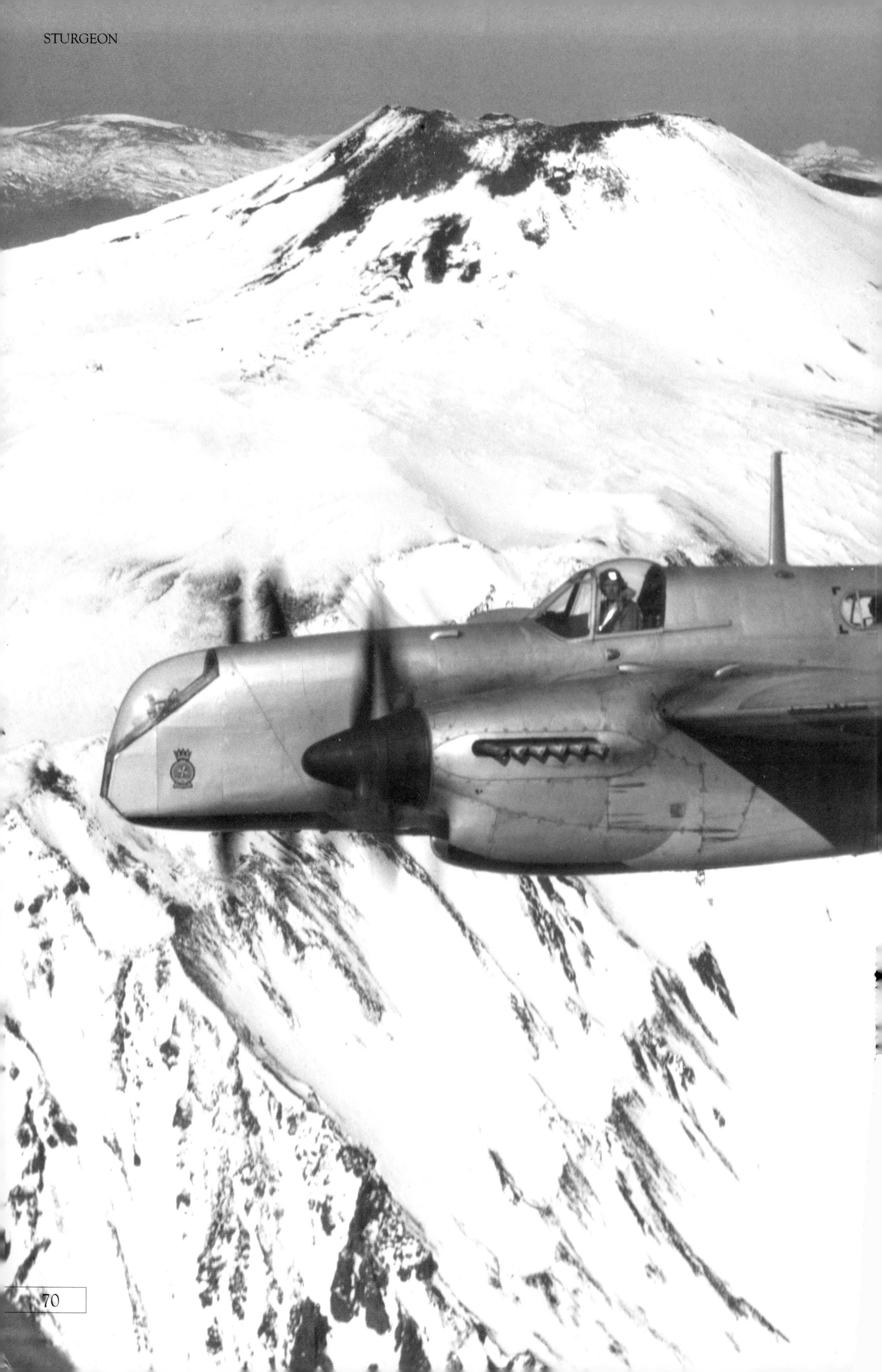

PULLING, NOT PUSHING

Air Station Photographic Officer and Senior 'O' of 728 Squadron. Lieutenant-Commander H. A. Monk DSM was the Squadron CO when he joined and Lieutenant-Commander P. C. S. Bagley succeeded him in February 1952. The Korean War was being fought throughout Commander Roberts's time at Hal Far (1951–53), and Malta became the main work-up base before the carriers and other ships deployed to the Far East, so it was an extremely busy place.

Having a dual rôle, and with a large Photographic Section to run, his duties as Senior 'O' of the Squadron meant that he had to divide his time between the two tasks and was kept fully occupied looking after both interests. He personally carried out all the aerial photography, using both Squadron and Station Flight aircraft, and took part in most of the Squadron's various flying tasks. A wide range of places was on the itinerary across the Mediterranean in support of the Fleet, and numerous types of aircraft were flown.

One of 728 Squadron's principal tasks was the provision of towed drogue and winged targets for the Fleet's air gunnery practice. Initially, the Squadron was equipped with the Mosquito Mk 39, which had been specially converted for target-towing, but in about March 1952 the first of the Sturgeon T.T. Mk 2s arrived and over the ensuing months the Shorts twin gradually replaced the de Havilland. By the time he left the Squadron in May 1953, Commander Roberts's log book records that in about fifty sorties he flew in Sturgeons TS478, '481, '485, '486, '488, '492, '493 and '495. He recalls:

> During my time on 728, the Squadron back-seat complement included, in addition to myself, four Commissioned or Senior Commissioned Observers (all ex TAGs [Telegraphist Air Gunners]) and three Tels (F) [Telegraphists (Flying)]. The observers provided navigator/WT operator expertise for the Mosquito and Expediter when these aircraft were used for mail collection and delivery and VIP passenger trips throughout the Mediterranean region. They also took their turn as winch operators on target-towing sorties. When the photographic marking of AA shoots was required, I used a Vinten K cine-camera in a second aircraft which positioned itself on the beam of the drogue or winged target. This enabled the shoot to be analysed by recording the position of the bursts in relation to the target on a circular, scaled (dart-board type) diagram which I then sent to the ship concerned. I also operated the drogue target in the photographic aircraft if the main target-towing aircraft went unserviceable so that the ship could still carry out a shoot (albeit without photographic marking). The Tels (F) were mostly employed as winch operators for the towed target sorties but were given navigation and photographic training on various other flights. When, in about January 1953, the Search and Rescue Flight (CO Lieutenant-Commander B. Paterson MBE DFC) was formed at Hal Far with two S-51 Dragonfly helicopters, the Tels (F) took on the duties of crewman/winchman.

As to the Sturgeon itself,

> I found the observer's navigation position [in the Sturgeon T.T.2] very spacious and comfortable, which greatly helped to make flying in the aircraft enjoyable. Vertical photography was carried out using a standard F.24 aerial camera installed in the underside of the aircraft. Photography from the nose position was a little more of a problem, as I discovered when I decided to take a cine recording from the nose during a mock torpedo attack on the Fleet. Take-off and landing with personnel in the nose position was not allowed, and the crew station had to be reached from the rear of the aircraft when airborne. This required the use of a very narrow tunnel along the bottom of the fuselage through which one had to pull oneself along head first on one's back with the help of handrails above. There was no room to carry a parachute, so a spare was placed in the nose position before take-off. Having unplugged the intercom and then sliding over half the length of the aircraft involved a few tense moments and fingers crossed that the pilot would not open the bomb-bay doors whilst his observer was in transit!
>
>   Target towing could get a bit 'dicey' if the odd AA burst was a little too close for comfort to the towing aircraft: 'I am towing the target, not pushing it!' was one of the standard messages sent to the ship concerned on such occasions.

Before streaming the drogue, it had to be secured to the winch wire by several turns of codline so as to provide about an eight-inch link of joining line which had to be cut with a curved 'Mae West' knife when the drogue was reeled in until the codline link was below the aircraft's open hatch ready for the drogue's release during a low flypast over the airfield at the end of the sortie. The objective was to release the drogue so that it fell clear of the aircraft and landed as close as possible to the personnel waiting to collect it, although this was not always successful. Landing a winged target safely on the runway was an even more difficult operation and targets were occasionally lost or damaged owing to poor timing.

Commander Graeme Rowan-Thomson joined 728 Squadron in May 1956 and flew his first Sturgeon sortie on 5 June following. He spent the remainder of the year at Hal Far and recalls thoroughly enjoyable times, flying many different aircraft types and undertaking a multitude of different tasks, notwithstanding the fact that the Suez Crisis erupted that autumn. His was a relatively short tour, but he managed to accumulate 82 hours on Sturgeons, almost all of them on Mk 3s. Flying them was the proverbial 'piece of cake':

> You lit up both engines, the contra-props rotated happily, making a lot of noise, taxying was simple (one could actually see the runway ahead!) and the take-off was straightforward because there was little or no tendency to swing. The tail came up at about 60 [knots] and we got airborne at around 90 or 95. Once in the air, we chuntered along at about 150 knots. We did not perform aerobatics: I do recall doing some slow barrel rolls on occasion, but I do not think that we would have made it to the top of a loop!

Most published sources state that the Sturgeons were replaced by Meteors in 1958 and while, indeed, Meteor T.T.20s did supplant the Shorts twins that year, Meteors had already been 'tugging' for some time as 728 Squadron utilised their T.7s for the purpose:

> In broad detail, the target could either be the aircraft itself, flown by the pilot, or a banner or a winged target towed by the aircraft. The first type or sortie was employed quite frequently for calibrating ships' gunnery radars or navigation radars, and, clearly, no live weapons were used. Meteors and Sturgeons were flown on both types of sortie, but the more popular mount was the Meteor because of its performance range although the Sturgeon would also be used without a tow if nothing spectacular was required. One major difference between the two aircraft was that the Sturgeon's winch, operated by the aircrewman in the rear cockpit, meant that the tow-line was adjustable; the Meteor had no such

Below: Sturgeon T.T. Mk 2s TS492 and, beyond, TS495 at Hal Far in 1953 or 1954. Mk 2s generally had call-signs (or 'side numbers') beginning '59' and following conversion to Mk 3 standards these tended to begin '58', but there were several exceptions; moreover, one particular call-sign was not necessarily permanently associated with one particular aircraft.

Left: A Sturgeon Mk 3 in 728 NAS colours. The quality of the image and the fact that the aircraft lacks a side number preclude positive identification, but the aircraft appears to be TS478. The yellow fuselage and upper-surface wing bands were standard markings throughout the Sturgeon fleet. It is easy to understand why many who worked with the Sturgeon 3 compared its lines with those of the Bristol Beaufighter.

FLEET AIR ARM MUSEUM

refinement and the whole length of the required tow had to be flaked out alongside the runway and yanked into the air following a steep climb on take-off. This violent treatment did not suit the drogue target, which really needed the more gentle run of the short tow on the Sturgeon winch followed by an extension to operating length when safely airborne.

Both these aircraft could be used to tow a banner, a four-foot-by-fourteen-foot canvas strip with a suitable metal towing arm at one end and a stabilising arm at the rear to stop the thing plunging all over the sky while under tow These could be used under 'dummy' conditions with no armament or under 'live' conditions when the ship, or attacking squadron aircraft, would fire 20mm cannon shells. If several aircraft were using the same target, then their rounds were coloured red, black, blue etc: and the colours totted up on landing. Ships would use banners, but normally only for their close-range pom-poms and without colouring the rounds although the heavyweight stuff—the standard Fleet 4.5-inch gun—would also sometimes make use of them. On its recovery at Hal Far, the banner, once released by the aircraft, would be gathered up and the hits physically counted, the results being conveyed back to the ship by radio. Rarely was a banner badly shredded following a shoot, and it was sometimes possible to tidy it up for re-use—which perhaps says something about the accuracy of the gunnery on particular occasions. However, to redress the balance, I have to say that I cannot recall my aircraft ever having been struck.

The targets were, as I remember, usually towed some 300–400 feet behind the Sturgeon. Although the winch was very reliable and never let me down, now and then a tow might be lost for some reason. The moment of detachment was always evident in the cockpit: the banner did cause noticeable drag, and if it were lost the Sturgeon would give a little 'jolt' forward. The target would be under fairly tight control—i.e., quite close to the towing aircraft—during take-off and initial climb, but it would be reeled out further once the Sturgeon had climbed a few hundred feet; our 'customers' were generally only a few miles offshore of Hal Far, so there was little time to waste. However, on arrival in the designated exercise area, the pilot would ring up the ship and ask for instructions concerning the length and distance of the tow, the range at which the aircraft was to operate, and whether off the beam or off the quarter, etc. The ship's commander was in overall command of the operation, and the only occasion on which the pilot might request termination was if he had an emergency (for example, the danger of running out of fuel).

The alternative target to the banner was the winged target. This was quite a technical piece of work and, whilst getting it airborne was straightforward, on the landing the Sturgeon pilot had to be talked down by the pilot in charge of the unit in an effort to get it back in one piece. Landing therefore called for extreme precision, although it often seemed to be the case that, no matter how accurately the aircraft was flown on the approach, the target ended up on the airfield as a pile of matchwood! Getting the target back down over the airfield could generally be accomplished smoothly, but, as soon as the tow was slipped, the target would tend to adopt a wild course of its own and come to rest somewhat the worse for wear—which, occurring with such frequency as it did, was very discouraging for the hard-working ground crews in attendance to retrieve it.

During Commander Rowan-Thomson's time at Hal Far, the veteran heavy cruiser HMS *Cumberland*, now employed as a trials ship, was a high priority for 728 Squadron to provide target facilities. The particular programme of the day was the Royal Navy's new suite of quick-firing guns that were to comprise the armament of the new *Tiger* class cruisers, and with which *Cumberland* had been temporarily equipped.

If *Cumberland* wanted a tow, she of course jolly well got a tow—the ship was in command and we did her bidding. We towed for her mostly 'on sleeve', but frequently just the aircraft were required. In the former cases, the sorties could be very tedious. There would generally be two Sturgeons, one towing a spare sleeve in case the first was shot down. One of the aircraft would be flying back and forth some six miles off the beam while the other circled perhaps ten miles away as a reserve. Thanks to the Sturgeon's endurance, this sort of thing could go on for four hours or more; indeed, there was a grave danger that pilots would fall asleep, and to counter this possibility I would change engines, or fly single-engined—with which the Sturgeon had absolutely no problems, of course. However, I nearly switched two engines off together on one occasion, while on another a plaintive voice came through the intercom, 'Sir, the drogue is about to hit the water!' as I drifted off to sleep and the aircraft gradually lost altitude.

Although the 'Flying Tels' had by 1956 mostly disappeared from Sturgeons, now and again we flew with an aircrewman in the back, and I remember that on one occasion, a photographic sortie, I had taxied out, taken off and climbed to about 500 feet when a small voice came from abaft, 'Sir, we have lost the camera.' It has slid out of the entry hatch in the belly of the aircraft! On another occasion—while the Suez operation was under way—I experienced an undercarriage failure; the leg would not retract properly. I had a tow at the time, and this was still on a short stay. When the leg finally behaved, I decided to ask the Tower to

Below: A close view of the nose of Sturgeon Mk 3 TS475. The box structure visible in the angle formed by the fuselage and propeller blades of the port engine is a small servicing platform, which is revealed more fully in the portrait of the aircraft that appears overleaf. Notice the very precise demarcation lines of the black and yellow under-surface paintwork.

have a look and prepared to fly by. I came along the runway, trailing this target but having quite forgotten that there was a US Army camp situated just off the end. Luckily the sleeve did minimal damage and the American colonel had a sense of humour, reminding us that we were fighting the Egyptians, not the Americans!

Lieutenant-Commander Andy Hamilton completed his twin conversion course at Culdrose before joining 801 Squadron (Sea Hornets), and he arrived on 728 Squadron at Hal Far early in 1956. During his first 'famil' flight in the Sturgeon, in March that year, he was immediately introduced to the single-engine flying capabilities of the aircraft when an engine overheated and its propellers had to be feathered. Generally, he says, the Sturgeon flew steadily and uneventfully, although in one respect 'it reminded me of my days flying the Sea Otter—push the stick to the left and five minutes later the aircraft decided to turn. It was a comfortable, "gentleman's aeroplane", however, and one ideally suited to the type of work we did. No beauty, but reliable.' During the build-up to the Suez campaign in the autumn of 1956, as well as target-towing and radar calibration, he was called upon to carry out a different sort of task—spotting for the guns of the fleet in the range just off the south-eastern coastline of Malta. 'My logbook contains references to many gunnery exercises—G.1, G.5, G.11, G.20, G.22, etc.'

In common with most of his colleagues on the Squadron, he found the actual task of towing to be undemanding, the most important attribute in a tug pilot being patience, although on one or two sorties the trundling backwards and forwards was enlivened when one of the gunners below hit the towing cable and severed the target. He continues:

> Amongst the ships utilising the towing facilities at this time were the destroyers *Chaplet*, *Duchess*, *Decoy* and *Diamond* and the cruiser *Birmingham*, as well as the trials cruiser *Cumberland*; the anti-submarine frigate (ex destroyer) *Ursa* and the fast minelayer *Manxman* were amongst those for which we also flew W/T sorties. We also did some low-level 'strikes' in the Sturgeons and Meteors against the carriers *Eagle* and *Bulwark*. When banner-towing for the carrier squadrons 800, 802, 897 and 899 Squadrons we flew the Meteors. We also managed to get all the Sturgeons up at one time for a formation flypast, I recall.

A perspective from below, on board HMS *Cumberland* when Sturgeons were towing, is provided by Sam Watson, who served on the ship from May 1955 until early 1957 and, as an Electrical Artificer 4th Class with a Petty Officer's rate, was involved with the fire control gunnery systems. These systems

> . . . were primarily linked to the single and twin 40mm Bofors mountings, the 4-inch and 4.5-inch mountings fitted on the port side amidships, the twin 3-inch

Below: Sturgeon T.T.3 TS475 under discussion by Short Brothers staff prior to re-delivery to the Royal Navy. All but the first of the conversions were carried out at the company's Rochester premises, and each aircraft took between six and nine months to re-equip, though the return to active service was sometimes further delayed. Each conversion, naturally, included a major overhaul.

Above: The personnel of 728 Squadron pose for an official photograph in 1957. Their backdrop is Sturgeon T.T. Mk 3 TS496. Even by the standards of the day, 728 had a very sizeable complement.

turret fitted in 'X' position and their associated radar tracking and fire control systems, MRS 8 and MRS 3.

I was specifically involved with the Gun Direction System that used the Type 901 early warning radar linked to GDS 5, which tracked targets at extreme range and directed the AA armament control systems directors automatically on to the target by transmitting bearing and tangent elevation for range. The MRS 3 (for the 3-inch turret) and MRS 8 (for the Bofors and 4-inch) radars would search rapidly in elevation for the target and then lock-on to it, whereupon the associated fire control system would compute the necessary training and elevation rates and aim-off for the weapons.

Tracer ammunition was used on the Bofors and proximity fuses on the 3-inch rounds to determine position accuracy. Sometimes a proximity burst would bring down the target. All shoots were filmed in colour. On one shoot I recall watching, the target was hit by a 3-inch shell, which brought it down, but the radar tracking system continued to track up the towing wire. There was a very hasty 'Check! Check! Check!' from the Air Direction Officer!

The twin 3-inch turret was not manned and was fully automatic from the magazine up to the breech, originally with a rate of fire of 180 rounds a minute (90 per barrel) although this was reduced to 120 to conserve ammunition and reduce wear on the barrels. The 3-inch turret used fixed ammunition and both barrels fired simultaneously. It was a formidable weapon.

A 6-inch turret was fitted in *Cumberland*'s 'B' position. This was essentially a surface weapon, controlled automatically by Box 10, a gunnery fire control system using data from radar or optical information of surface targets. It did, however, have an anti-aircraft capability and its rate of fire was 24 rounds a minute (twelve per barrel).

One of the interesting points about the ship is that it was fitted with eight hydraulically driven underwater vanes (four each side), similar to a submarine's hydroplanes. A reference gyroscope provided the horizontal datum, and in this way *Cumberland* became a stabilised platform for the gunnery systems. However, during gunnery tracking trials, a simple harmonic motion signal was fed into the stabiliser system in place of the gyro reference and this caused the stabilisers to rotate differentially, much like ailerons on an aircraft, inducing a roll motion to the ship, the roll angle dependent upon the speed of the ship. Thus, during trials with aircraft, the radar tracking systems were required to maintain a lock on the target despite the heavy roll on the ship. The start of this routine was a pipe which announced, typically, 'The ship will be force-rolled in five minutes' time!' *Cumberland* would roll quite suddenly and quickly to about 30 degrees or so, dwell for a few seconds then roll in the opposite direction, and this motion would continue for a considerable time, presumably until the tracking trials were completed for that aircraft sortie. Apparently, from the air, the spectacle of a 10,000-ton cruiser rolling so violently at speed was quite awe-inspiring. On board, walking anywhere on the ship was extremely uncomfortable, particularly from forward to aft or *vice-versa*, and one would be thrown quite forcibly from one side to the other. From our point of view, the experience of the ship rolling about whilst the gun barrels appeared to be stationary was very odd indeed—but it proved the effectiveness of the stabilisation system.

Short Sturgeon T. T. Mk 3 Conversions

Aircraft	Commenced	Completed	Remarks
TS475	January 1954	May 1954	Prototype conversion.
TS476	November 1955	1956	Returned to 728 NAS.
TS477	May 1954	October 1954	Returned to 728 NAS as '584'.
TS478	September 1954	January 1955	Returned to 728 NAS as '598'.
TS479	October 1955	January 1957	Not returned to service.
TS480	January 1956	1957	Not returned to service.
TS481	September 1955	June 1956	Returned to 728 NAS as '582'.
TS482	November 1953	March 1955	Fate uncertain.
TS483	May 1954	December 1954	Returned to 728 NAS as '585'.
TS484	April 1955	November 1955	Returned to 728 NAS.
TS485	January 1955	October 1955	Returned to 728 NAS.
TS486	February 1955	December 1955	Returned to 728 NAS.
TS487	–	–	Not converted (crashed 1951).
TS488	October 1953	January 1955	Returned to 728 NAS as '581'.
TS489	–	–	Not converted (lost 1951).
TS490	February 1954	August 1954	Returned to 728 NAS as '588'.
TS491	–	–	Not converted (employed at RNAS Ford etc, on general duties).
TS492	May 1955	January 1956	Returned to 728 NAS as '587'.
TS493	May 1953	June 1954	Returned to 728 NAS as '586'.
TS494	–	–	Not converted (lost 1952).
TS495	May 1953	April 1956	Returned to 728 NAS as '587' (later '583').
TS496	February 1954	July 1954	Returned to 728 NAS as '582'.
TS497	May 1955	October 1956	Not returned to service.

All these systems were subsequently fitted to HM Ships *Blake*, *Tiger* and *Lion*, the last of the Royal Navy's 'conventional' cruisers.

Commander David Corkhill DSC, who commanded 728 Squadron at Hal Far throughout 1954, recalls that the Sturgeon was a vast improvement over the Mosquito, despite the latter's legendary status as a fighter and a bomber; nobody liked the Mosquito as a 'target-tugger'. He was CO during the phased changeover from the long-nose Sturgeon Mk 2 to the short-nose Mk 3, and his log book shows that, at various times, he was at the controls of TS475, '478, '480, '481, '485, '486, '493, '495 and '496 and that Tels (F) Mann, Morley and Webb, Petty Officer Lapping and Aircrewmen Collyer and Homer—all extremely experienced people—accompanied him on some of the flights.

The Mk 3 handled even more pleasantly in the air than its predecessor, as Commander Corkhill remembers:

> The T.T.3 was a much nicer aircraft; we had imagined that the Mk 2 could not be improved upon, but the Mk 3 succeeded in being a better aeroplane. It was faster and smoother, and the view forward, without the extended nose, was better; it was a most comfortable aeroplane to fly, with everything in the right place for the pilot. Landing was a joy—in fact, I have never landed a more comfortable aircraft. The approach speed was gentle, and the 'bounce' on touching down barely perceptible.

As in later years, a good deal of the Squadron's work in 1954 was undertaken in conjunction with HMS *Cumberland*, the Royal Navy's gunnery trials ship,

> . . . not only towing but also radar calibration, for which we flew our Vampires and Sea Hornets as well as our Sturgeons. This work was frequently carried out very early in the morning—and indeed, in Sturgeons, sometimes at night, aided by

the fact that the aircraft had a handy light beneath it and a Morse key right by the pilot's side so that transmissions could be made both by voice and by signal. Telegraphists were not often carried on board the aircraft for these particular tasks, although there would always be an observer, whose duties included the operation of the winch gear if we were towing.

There were frequent breaks in routine, for example an occasion when I had to fly to Catania and another when I attended the submarine HMS *Sentinel* close inshore in Aranci Bay, Sardinia, the vessel somewhat stricken with engine trouble and requiring a spare part. An inflatable dinghy was stowed in the aircraft, and after I had conducted a low pass over the submarine to check my approach, it was dropped nearby. Thanks to the ingenuity of the Squadron Safety Officer, the dinghy had been rigged with an extemporary line so that it would inflate as it left the aircraft, the precious engine part secured within. The component was successfully delivered, perfectly dry, and *Sentinel* was able to carry out repairs and continue on her way. The event caused much interest throughout the Squadron.

My only 'moment' in a Sturgeon was when, during a flight back to Lee-on-Solent in a Mk 2, I stopped en route at Istres in France but had to carry out a flapless landing because of a problem with the hydraulics. Luckily I had taken the precaution of making sure that I was accompanied on the flight by AA2 Watson, who rectified the fault in record time.

728 was a most enjoyable appointment—for all concerned, including also the people from the Instrument Test Flight, who were stationed at Hal Far with us. The wide variety of aircraft available, and the differing tasks to be undertaken, meant that there was never any monotony. Aircraft were circulated amongst the aircrews as much as possible, and so we became an extremely versatile unit.

One last memory. Few people had the experience of landing a Sturgeon on board an aircraft carrier. It was something I had always wanted to do, and although I never actually managed it I did come very close on one occasion. One of our carriers was off Malta, and I decided to make an approach with my undercarriage down. The ship was happy to join in the fun and I prepared for a dummy deck landing, receiving, of course, a wave-off as I drew near the round-down, whereupon I opened up and flew away, waggling my wings in thanks. A

Below: Most of the Sturgeon pilots had cut their 'twin-engine teeth' on the de Havilland Mosquito, and a number of them had experience of the target-towing version of that aircraft, the T.T. Mk 39, an example of which, PF606, is depicted. However, this variant—the last of a very distinguished design—proved to be widely disliked by its pilots, so much so that a Maintenance Test Pilot at one of the Royal Navy's air stations point blank refused to fly it. One of its less endearing tendencies was a violent swing on take-off—not the sort of manœuvre required with a target in tow; indeed, it was not unknown for the aircraft to 'swap ends' during its take-off run.

shame that I could not have carried it through—the Sturgeon was so responsive and the view ahead was so good . . . !

Virtually every production Sturgeon flew with 728 Squadron at some time, only TS482, TS487, TS489 and TS491 apparently missing out. Examples were TS478 as '598/HF', TS481 ('590/HF'), TS485 ('592/HF'), TS488 as a T.T. Mk 3 ('581/HF') and TS493 also as a Mk 3 ('586/HF'). 'HF' refers of course to Hal Far, but the letters were not necessarily carried by every aircraft based there. From March 1958 the T.T. Mk 3 was gradually replaced by the T.T. Mk 20 version of the Gloster Meteor, and the last Sturgeons were retired in October of that year; it would have been earlier had not the Meteors experienced some difficulties with their towing winches. The last operational flight took place on 1 October, when TS485 was flown by Lieutenant Commander 'Cue' Cureton, but it ended somewhat ignominiously as the Sturgeon's undercarriage collapsed just as it was taxying to a halt! Most of the Sturgeons had by this time either been scrapped (at nearby Kalafrana or back in Britain) or sent to Aircraft Holding Units; the few remaining were rapidly disposed of thereafter.

Finally, a fighter pilot's viewpoint. Captain Alan Leahy CBE DSC, one of the Royal Navy's most experienced pilots of the postwar era, had the opportunity to fly a Sturgeon, as he relates:

It was way back in the 'good old days'—in 1954 to be exact—and 801 Squadron's Sea Furies had disembarked to RNAS Hal Far in Malta. In the bar one evening, a friend of mine asked me if, having been an old Sea Hornet pilot, I would like to have a trip in one of 728 Squadron's Sturgeons. Well, why not? Next morning, after a quick brief on the basics, I found myself looking up at this rather ugly machine, much taller than the Sea Hornet, but with two Merlins like the Sea Hornet to reassure me I climbed aboard. Two or three years before this I had occasionally air-tested the Mosquito Mk 39 at Culdrose (the Maintenance Test Pilot refused to fly them). The Mk 39 was a modified Mosquito designed to tow targets. It did not leap into the air in a joyous fashion but lumbered, and with one engine feathered there was a gradual loss of height which made one wary of feathering one in case it could not be unfeathered again. So I was interested to find out how the Sturgeon compared.

There was no swing on take-off, which could catch the unwary in the Mosquito, but neither was there a swing in the Sea Hornet which was not blessed with the complication of two engines fitted with contra-rotating propellers. The flight only lasted forty-five minutes, however, so there was not a lot one could find out. The Sturgeon could fly on one engine without losing height, it could do a barrel roll without getting upset and it was easy to handle in the circuit. What else can one say about it? Not much. I never had the opportunity to fly one again—nor, it must be said, did that cause me any concern!

Below: A poor-quality photograph of TS481 following its conversion to a T.T. Mk 3. Neither the date nor the location can be confirmed (although are believed to be 1957 and RNAS Lossiemouth), but the aircraft is still, apparently, fully equipped and the picture is interesting for the fact that it shows the enlarged presentation of the 'Royal Navy' legend that was introduced to Fleet Air Arm aircraft in the late 1950s, in this instance in twelve-inch-high characters instead of the original four-inch (which the serial number here retains). A Westland Wyvern strike fighter is parked alongside.

Colours and Markings

A Selection of Short Sturgeon Paint Schemes

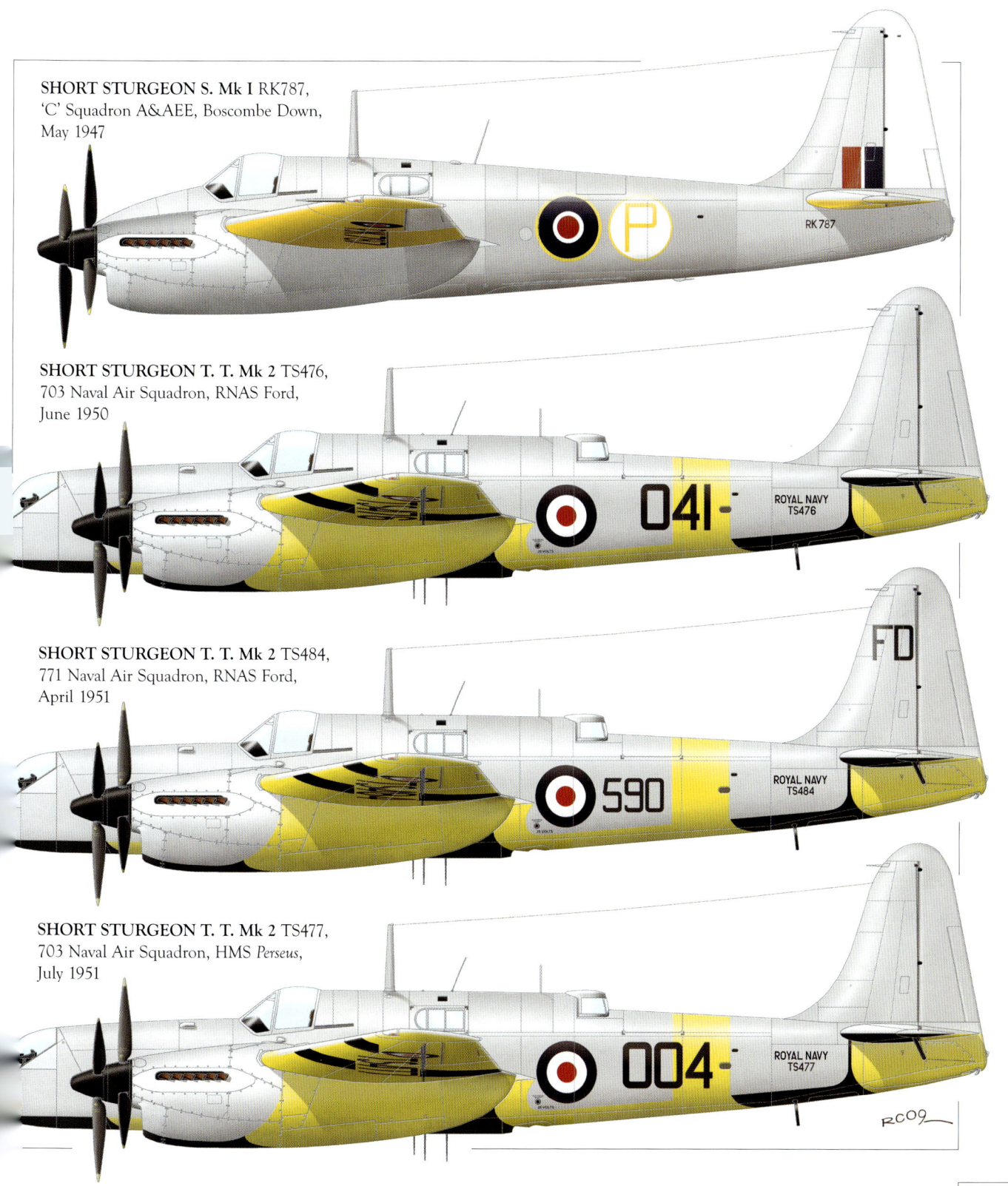

SHORT STURGEON S. Mk I RK787, 'C' Squadron A&AEE, Boscombe Down, May 1947

SHORT STURGEON T. T. Mk 2 TS476, 703 Naval Air Squadron, RNAS Ford, June 1950

SHORT STURGEON T. T. Mk 2 TS484, 771 Naval Air Squadron, RNAS Ford, April 1951

SHORT STURGEON T. T. Mk 2 TS477, 703 Naval Air Squadron, HMS *Perseus*, July 1951

STURGEON

SHORT STURGEON T. T. Mk 2
TS492, 728 Naval Air Squadron, RNAS Hal Far,
December 1952

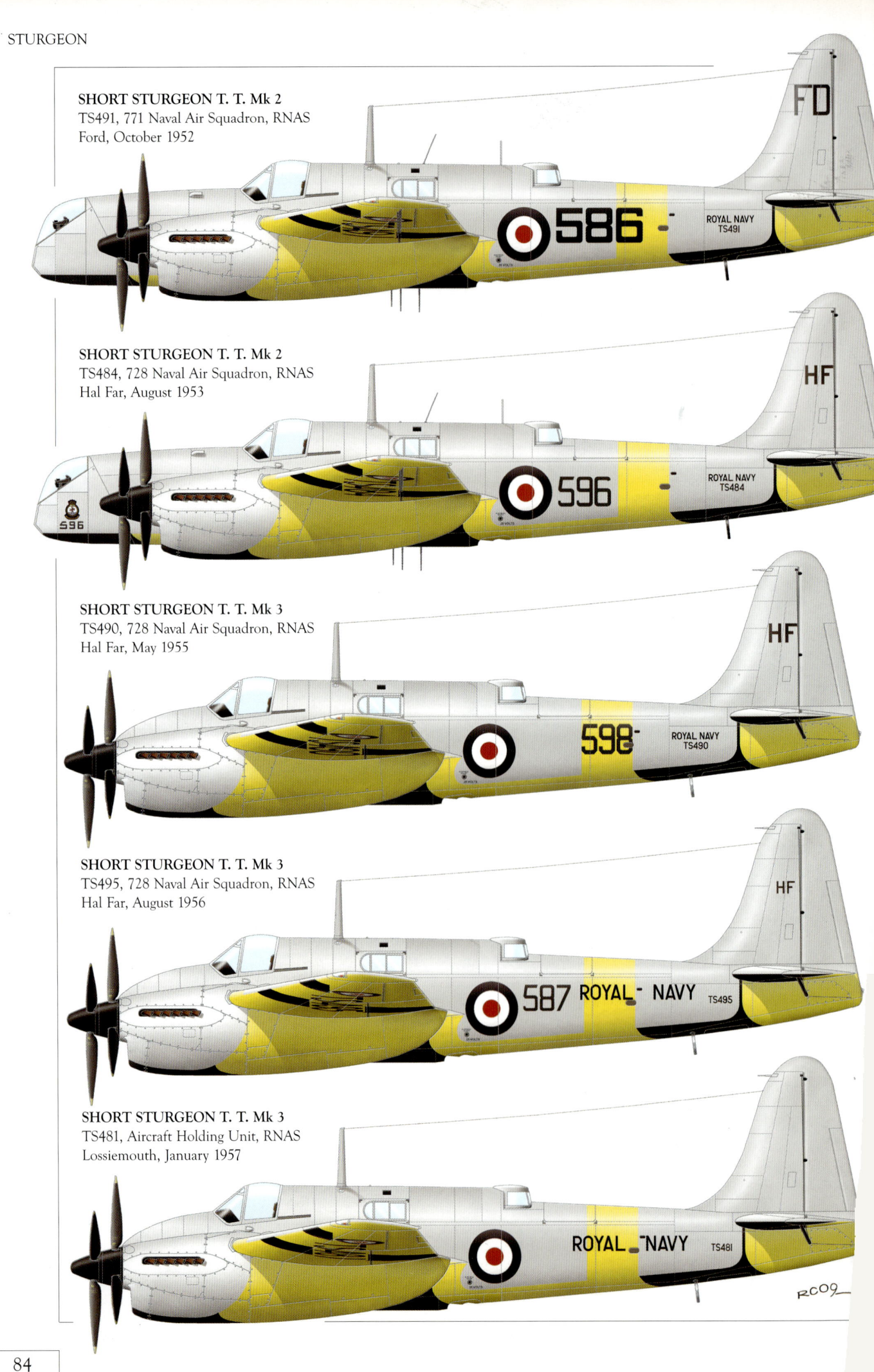

STURGEON

SHORT STURGEON T. T. Mk 2
TS491, 771 Naval Air Squadron, RNAS
Ford, October 1952

SHORT STURGEON T. T. Mk 2
TS484, 728 Naval Air Squadron, RNAS
Hal Far, August 1953

SHORT STURGEON T. T. Mk 3
TS490, 728 Naval Air Squadron, RNAS
Hal Far, May 1955

SHORT STURGEON T. T. Mk 3
TS495, 728 Naval Air Squadron, RNAS
Hal Far, August 1956

SHORT STURGEON T. T. Mk 3
TS481, Aircraft Holding Unit, RNAS
Lossiemouth, January 1957